SEAPORT AND AIRPORT

INFRASTRUCTURE ECONOMICS AND POLICY - A SINGAPORE PERSPECTIVE

Ho Kim Hin/David

PARTRIDGE

Copyright © 2020 by Ho Kim Hin/David.

ISBN: Hardcover   978-1-5437-6060-6
         Softcover   978-1-5437-6058-3
         eBook   978-1-5437-6059-0

All rights reserved. No part of this book may be used or reproduced by any means, graphic, electronic, or mechanical, including photocopying, recording, taping or by any information storage retrieval system without the written permission of the author except in the case of brief quotations embodied in critical articles and reviews.

Because of the dynamic nature of the Internet, any web addresses or links contained in this book may have changed since publication and may no longer be valid. The views expressed in this work are solely those of the author and do not necessarily reflect the views of the publisher, and the publisher hereby disclaims any responsibility for them.

Print information available on the last page.

To order additional copies of this book, contact
Toll Free +65 3165 7531 (Singapore)
Toll Free +60 3 3099 4412 (Malaysia)
orders.singapore@partridgepublishing.com

www.partridgepublishing.com/singapore

CONTENTS

Foreword vii
Acknowledgements xi
About The Authors xiii
Introduction xv

Chapter 1   The Seaport Economy – The Policy Experience of Singapore 1

Chapter 2   Risk Management In Large Physical Infrastructure Investment: The Context of Seaport Infrastructure Development and Investment ... 24

Chapter 3   Structural Dynamics in the Policy Planning of Large Infrastructural Investment under the Competitive Environment – The Context of Seaport Throughput and Capacity 68

Chapter 4   The Global Outreach of the Port of Singapore Pivotal and Its Modest Origin 106

Chapter 5   The Airport Economy – The Singapore Challenge 115

Chapter 6   The Conclusion & References 153

FOREWORD

"Over 100 years ago, this was a mud-flat, swamp. Today, this is a modern city. Ten years from now, this will be a metropolis. Never fear."

(The first Prime Minister of Singapore Lee Kuan Yew, 1965)

This book highlights the findings, contributions and recommendations made on several crucial issues concerning the concomitant subjects of large and complex physical infrastructural provision like the seaport and the airport. Chapter 1 takes a close look at the seaports, where ships, cargoes, cranes, forklifts and storage yards, warehouses, lorries, roads and rail lines abound. Cargo handling has evolved to become a lot more complex that require elegant solutions, which can only be put together with specialist knowledge. Such knowledge is encompassed within a concept of supply chain management (SCM). SCM is essential to enable Singapore to develop into a global integrated logistics hub, i.e. global gateway.

Chapter 2 reiterates that the growth of developing countries depends very much on having adequate physical infrastructure to support economic development. As a strategic response, many physical infrastructure investments like seaports are being privatised and highly purpose built. The Chapter examines the merits of viable seaport infrastructure investment, typically 'lumpy' and requiring large capital expenditure and long payback period. A key feature of such an infrastructure investment is to structure a defensible risk management strategy to deal with uncertainties. This risk management strategy can offer responsive alternatives to new opportunities. Singapore's Jurong Port is the case study.

Chapter 3 is concerned with the growth of developing countries ., which depends very much on having adequate physical infrastructure to support economic development. As a strategic response, many physical infrastructure investments like seaports are being privatised and highly purpose built. The Chapter examines the merits of viable seaport infrastructure investment, typically 'lumpy' and requiring large capital expenditure and long pay-back period. A key feature of such an infrastructure investment is to structure a defensible risk management strategy to deal with uncertainties. Such a defensible risk management strategy can offer responsive alternatives to new opportunities. Singapore's Jurong Port is the case study. The risk management strategy is analysed and it deploys risk simulation for scenario planning in conjunction with constraint optimisation. This risk management strategy finds that it is more defensible to configure Jurong Port, and a seaport in general, into the maritime industrial and logistics park (MILP).

Chapter 4 is concerned with the global outreach of the small island state of Singapore's seaport operation, owing to its limited land area of a mere 724 sq. km (280 sq. miles) and its small population size of about 5.7 million by 2019 (according to the Department of Statistics, Ministry of Trade & Industry, Singapore). Such limiting considerations constrain Singapore's seaport available cargo throughput. To overcome this small island state's limiting growth prospects, it is essential to grow and sustain the global outreach of the Port of Singapore. The late Sir Stamford Raffles, with great strategic foresight, took possession of the then unimportant and insignificant island state of Singapore. He envisaged that Singapore would become a significant trading port that would well serve the interests of Britain. His vision has largely panned out to be true.

Last but not least, Chapter 5 recognizes that for financial instruments investing like that of common stocks, bonds, direct and indirect real estate, both the technical and fundamental analyses are conducted to offer a reference for decision makers. Likewise, and in public physical infrastructure developments like Singapore's global Changi Airport, public funding is also a form of investment that entails uncertainties, which need to be rigorously evaluated with financial modelling on the risks and returns. Public physical infrastructural investing like Singapore's global Changi Airport also seeks to pursue crucial expansion and a larger strategic objective for the long-term, well-being of the nation. Singapore's global Changi Airport is not just a public infrastructure but also a key pillar of strength to support the growth of Singapore's trade-oriented market economy.

Happy reading.

Yours sincerely,
Professor (Dr) HO, Kim Hin / David
Singapore
November 2020.

ACKNOWLEDGEMENTS

The author wishes to extend his most sincere appreciation to the School of Design & Environment, under the highly able Deanship of the Provost & Chair Professor (Dr) LAM Khee Poh, of the National University of Singapore. The same wish is extended to the University of Cambridge and the University of Hertfordshire in Hatfield, UK. These three tertiary institutions of higher learning and research are globally leading Universities, inspiring and encouraging both modern and contemporary studies of large and complex physical infrastructural provision, in particularly the seaport and the airport.

ABOUT THE AUTHORS

Dr HO Kim Hin / David is Honorary Professor in Development Economics & Land Economy, awarded by the UK public university, the University of Hertfordshire. He retired end-May 2019 as Professor (Associate) (Tenured) from the National University of Singapore. Professor HO spent the last thirty-one years across several sectors, which include the military, oil refining, aerospace engineering, public housing, resettlement, land acquisition, land reclamation, real estate investment, development and international real estate investing. He spent six years in the real estate career as part of the executive management group of Singapore Technologies at Pidemco Land Limited, and as part of the senior management team of the Government of Singapore Investment Corporation's GIC Real Estate Private Limited. Seventeen years are spent in the National University of Singapore at the then School of Building and Estate Management, the Department of Real Estate, School of Design and Environment, where his research expertise is in two areas.

First is international real estate in the area of risk-return behavior behind international real estate investing in direct and indirect real estate. Secondly, is urban and public policy analysis involving real estate, sea transport, public housing, land and land use. Schooled in development economics and in land economy at the University of Cambridge, England, he has effectively extended these disciplines to examine his two expertise areas. Apart from being well versed in econometrics, his quantitative interests include real estate demand and supply, investment and finance, artificial intelligent modeling in real estate and system dynamics modeling for real estate market analysis and public policy analysis. He is the Member of the Royal Economics Society (U.K.), Academic Member of the National Council of Real Estate Investment Fiduciaries (U.S.), Fellow of the American Real Estate Society (U.S.), member of the American Economic Association (U.S.) and member of the Economic Society of Singapore and the Singapore Institute of Management. He holds the degrees of Master of Philosophy (1st Class Honors with Distinction), Honorary Doctor of Letters and the Doctor of Philosophy from the University of Cambridge, U.K. He has published widely in top international journals and conferences, in chapters of international academic book publishers. Dr Ho has written 12 major books (including this book), undertaken many consultancies and funded research projects. He has written a total of about 275 published works (with 91 in peer reviewed, reputable international journals). He is an editorial board member of the Journal of Economics & Public Finance, Real Estate Economics journal, Journal of Property Research, Journal of Property Investment & Finance, Journal of Real Estate Finance & Economics, the Property Management journal and the International Journal of Strategic Property Management. He has published widely in conferences, Finance, chapters of international academic book publishers, undertaken many consultancies and funded research projects. He is an immediate past Governor of the St Gabriel's Foundation that oversees nine schools in Singapore; and a District Judge equivalent member of the Valuation Review Board, Ministry of Finance, Singapore, and the Singapore Courts.

INTRODUCTION

Seaport and Airport Infrastructure Economics and Policy - A Singapore Perspective

Chapter 1 reiterates that the seaport is originally conceived for ships to berths. Ships bring cargoes from the place or origin to their eventual destinations. Over time, the seaport would grow in complexity. This is because small lots of cargoes from different shippers need to be consolidated at the warehouse before they are loaded into containers bound for different destinations. As technology advances and consumer preferences changes, the variety of raw materials, semi-finished products and manufactured goods have also increased. Some of these cargoes are perishables that need to be handled in a cold chain to be delivered within a certain time line. Others, like project cargoes may be outsized that cannot be packaged within standard containers and need to be handled differently. In addition, there could also be cargoes that are in dry or liquid bulk form, or are categorised as hazardous that need to be handled with different methods, equipment, facilities or in accordance with certain statutory regulations. In the early days, cargo handling involved primarily the transportation of goods.

Accordingly, at the seaports, you can find only ships, cranes, some forklifts, and storage yards in some warehouses or open space. Cargo handling has evolved to become a lot more complex that require elegant solutions that can only be put together with specialised knowledge. Such specialised knowledge is encompassed within a concept of supply chain management (SCM). SCM is essential to enable Singapore to develop into a global integrated logistics hub, i.e. global gateway. Beyond transportation and cargo handling per se, SCM is a concept that incorporates components of services within the entire logistics value chain to offer customers a complete "end-to-end" service from suppliers to end customers. Accordingly, instead of the shippers or consignees having to source and decide how the cargoes are to be transported, which shipping or airlines to use, which port or airport to go to, as well as various other details, they would appoint operators in the SCM to handle all these for them. In recognition of the specialist knowledge required, there is a global trend of rising preference by companies to opt for integrative SCM outsourcing models. This will invariably entail the co-ordination and transfer of three flows i.e. the cargoes themselves, the associated information that communicate the nature of the cargoes and where they may be at any one point in time, and the funds required to be paid to the different service providers in the value chain to effect the movements and transfers.

Chapter 2 reiterates that the growth of developing countries depends very much on having adequate physical infrastructure to support economic development. As a strategic response, many physical infrastructure investments like seaports are being privatised and highly purpose built. The Chapter examines the merits of viable seaport infrastructure investment, typically 'lumpy' and requiring large capital expenditure and long payback period. A key feature of such an infrastructure investment is to structure a defensible risk management strategy to deal with uncertainties. This risk management strategy can offer responsive alternatives to new opportunities. Singapore's Jurong Port is the case study. The risk management strategy is analysed, and deploys risk simulation for scenario planning in conjunction with constraint optimisation. This original risk management strategy finds that it is more defensible to configure Jurong Port, and a seaport in general, into the maritime industrial and logistics park (MILP) instead of the higher-margin and purpose-built container terminal strategy, which is inherently volatile (i.e. uncertain or risky). The planned scenarios and their projections, under the risk management strategy are then compared with the consequential developments in reality. The results highlight that the sustained viability of Jurong Port is attributed to the risk management strategy.

Chapter 3 is concerned with the growth of developing countries., which depends very much on having adequate physical infrastructure to support economic development. As a strategic response, many physical infrastructure investments like seaports are being privatised and highly purpose built. The Chapter examines the merits of viable seaport infrastructure investment, typically 'lumpy' and requiring large capital expenditure and long pay-back period. A key feature of such an infrastructure investment is to structure a defensible risk management strategy to deal with uncertainties. Such a defensible risk management strategy can offer responsive alternatives to new opportunities. Singapore's Jurong Port is the case study. The risk management strategy is analysed and it deploys risk simulation for scenario planning in conjunction with constraint optimisation. This risk management strategy finds that it is more defensible to configure Jurong Port, and a seaport in general, into the maritime industrial and logistics park (MILP), instead of the higher-margin and purpose-built container terminal strategy, which is inherently volatile (i.e. uncertain or risky). The planned scenarios and their projections, under the original risk management strategy are then compared with the consequential developments in reality. The results highlight that the sustained viability of Jurong Port is attributed to its risk management strategy.

Chapter 4 is concerned with the global outreach of the small island state of Singapore's seaport operation, owing to its limited land area of a mere 724 sq. km (280 sq. miles) and its small population size of about 5.7 million by 2019 (according to the Department of Statistics, Ministry of Trade & Industry, Singapore). Such vital limiting considerations constrain Singapore's seaport available cargo throughput. To overcome this small island state's limiting growth prospects, it is essential to grow and sustain the global outreach of the Port of Singapore. The late Sir Stamford Raffles, with great strategic foresight, took possession of the then unimportant and insignificant island state of Singapore. He envisaged that Singapore would become a significant trading port that would well serve the interests of Britain. His vision has largely panned out to be true. Today, Singapore is no longer a colony of Britain. Singapore is an interdependent sovereign island state. Britain is no longer a colonial master. Yet, both countries remain close friends and strategic partners whereby their future relationship would continue to be founded on their historical bond and shaped by the alignment of their strategic interests in the global new order. Indeed, the British maritime legacy in Singapore should not be confined to some maritime museums. Such a legacy should be leveraged upon as the basis to create value and improve the lives the peoples of both countries and globally. There is tremendous scope for public and private sectors' participation from both countries to form strategic and business alliances, based on the vision and the meaningful of the 'Framework for Strategic Maritime Collaboration'.

Lastly, Chapter 5 recognises that for financial instruments investing like that of common stocks, bonds, direct and indirect real estate, both the technical and fundamental analyses are often conducted to offer a reference for decision makers. Likewise, and in public physical infrastructure developments like the Singapore global Changi Airport, public funding is also a form of investment that entails uncertainties, which need to be rigorously evaluated with financial modelling on the risks and returns. Beyond financial returns, public physical infrastructural investing like Singapore's global Changi Airport seeks to pursue a larger strategic objective for the long-term, well-being of the nation. Singapore's global Changi Airport is not just a public infrastructure but also a key pillar of strength to support the growth of Singapore's trade-oriented market economy. Beyond airport development *per se*, the provision for the expansion of Singapore's global Changi Airport with its third and fourth runways, would eventuate significant contribution to Singapore's urban renewal and development. While the third runway would primarily be for civil aviation in conjunction with the development of terminal T5, the fourth runway would be for the eventual relocation of the RSAF Paya Lebar Air Base to the Changi East district. When the T5 and fourth runway developments materialise, this would free up some 800 ha of land, currently occupied by the RSAF Paya Lebar Air Base, is meant for housing, industry, recreation and other uses. The additional freed up land of 800 ha of land would enable Singapore's Urban Redevelopment Authority (URA) to liberalise the height restrictions around the Paya Lebar district, currently necessary to facilitate military air operations. Consequently, a lot of more urban redevelopment projects can be so planned and undertaken, to safeguard an even cleaner, greener, much less noisy, mixed-use built environment for Singaporeans; and to create more space for industrial and economic developments.

The Civil Aviation Authority of Singapore (CAAS) is the body in charge of the developments and operations of airports in Singapore before 2009. Thereafter, the business aspects of the CAAS is corporatized to form the Changi Airport Group (CAG). Beyond managing the Changi Airport *per se*, CAG also invests in and manages foreign airports through its subsidiary Changi Airports International (CAI). CAI's goal is to build a quality portfolio of airport investments worldwide with strong markets and significant development potential. Key CAI business activities include investments in airports, the provision of consultancy and airport management services. Today, CAI's foot print include the major economies of China, India, the Middle East and Europe. Chapter 5 demonstrates how the development of the airport performance model (APM) on the basis of economic conceptions and the principles of system modelling, can be readily adopted to support scenario planning and policy analysis. The airport performance model (APM) would be beneficial to policy makers and investors by providing them with a structured framework to consider the questions they are seeking to answer, and the decisions that they would need to make.

It is acknowledged that the APM can potentially be expanded to include more factors, and to deal with more complexities. Chapter 5 offers a preliminary platform to stimulate research endeavours in public policy analysis, especially in projecting future performance of physical transport infrastructural provision, within the context of portfolio management and its resource constrained optimisation. Actual economic data can also be inputted into such models for scenarios generation to support policy development and decision making. Such big data analysis and scenario planning should open up a wide field for policy research, by way of reinforcing loop(s) to contribute towards making Singapore a knowledge and research centre for the aviation and aerospace sector.

CHAPTER 1

THE SEAPORT ECONOMY – THE POLICY EXPERIENCE OF SINGAPORE

The unique challenge faced by both Singapore and Hong Kong is that both are small cities with limited populations, land resources and small manufacturing bases. Notwithstanding such a challenge, Singapore and Hong Kong haves been recognised as leading seaport cities of the world. However, their growths as seaport cities are inundated with persistently battling odds and difficulties. Singapore and Hong Kong face the similar constraint where the supply of land is scarce. In Singapore, its problem is even aggravated with limited water front to build berths and sea space for ships to manoeuvre. Unlike Singapore, Hong Kong opens out to the South China sea without constraint. Singapore's seaport operations are constrained by the busy and relatively narrow Straits of Singapore, bounded by Indonesia's Batam archipelago and barely 20 km to the south.

Whilst land is a critical scarce resource for seaport development, there is competition for alternative economic generating uses for e.g. housing, commercial, or industrial activities. Such a land resource dilemma is an even more complex issue if one takes into consideration the progressive transformation of Singapore and Hong Kong into essentially tertiary economies each. For Singapore, it has only a small population of about 5 to 6 million people, and its manufacturing sector constitutes less than a quarter of its economy. Hong Kong's tertiary economy is even more challenging. Its manufacturing sector has substantively relocated to neighbouring Shenzhen and other parts of China, where land, labour, capital and entrepreneurship are more abundantly available and competitive. As a result, the induced demand for seaport services to handle container, physical and bulk goods, originating from or destined for Singapore and Hong Kong *per se*, have inevitably limited growth prospects or to decline over time. Such limiting growth prospects in turn constrains both their seaports' available cargo throughput.

Recognising the foregoing constraints affecting domestic generated seaport throughput, Singapore and Hong Kong have each developed sizeable transhipment traffic. For Singapore, transhipment traffic refers to goods that are brought into Singapore by mainline vessels from Europe and North American, for subsequent transfer into feeder vessels that bring the goods or cargoes to eventual destinations of the smaller seaports in Asia. Similarly, exports from neighbouring countries may also bring to Singapore for transhipment to eventual destinations in Europe or North America. Hong Kong largely serves as the transhipment hub for cargoes flowing between China and Europe. The foregoing initiatives are relatively successful. Indeed, transhipment cargoes constitute in excess of 80% and 60% of seaport throughput for Singapore and Hong Kong respectively. Both Singapore and Hong Kong are recognised as leading transhipment hubs in the world for years, particularly in the 1990s, and prior to the influx of massive investments and exponential growth of seaports in China from year 2000s onwards.

However, the global transhipment business is relatively uncertain and volatile when compared with domestically generated throughput in which demand is relatively inelastic. For instance, and regardless of the price of Singapore's seaport services, automobiles that are imported for use in Singapore need to be unloaded at Singapore's seaport. Likewise, manufactured goods from Singapore also need to be exported through its seaport. Transhipment traffic itself can be diverted to alternative seaports for transhipment fairly easily, usually in response to changes in the price of seaport services or congestion that lead to delays. Products from Europe and destined for China may be transhipped in Singapore or neighbouring Malaysia's Klang seaport. As such, while domestic seaport throughput provides the basic demand or the base load for sustaining the transhipment business, there is also the opportunity for throughput growth. Small economies like Singapore and Hong Kong re no exceptions.

The successful transhipment hub business for Singapore and Hong Kong are due in no small part to the extensive and intensive physical infrastructure that they have invested. It must be acknowledged that they both developed their seaports with a proactive transhipment strategy that serve their associated hinterlands. The emerging South East (SE) Asian region as Singapore's hinterland and developing China as Hong Kong's hinterland, did not offer substantial seaport demand competition then. Indeed, whilst the mainline shipping services from Europe and North America formed a hub at the seaports of Singapore and Hong Kong, the hub offered comprehensive feeder services to facilitate onward connections to the respective hinterlands of SE Asia and China. Therefore, Singapore and Hong Kong have enjoyed first movers' advantage by filling the void in seaport demand competition, made themselves useful and thrived.

Fast forward to the 21st century, these SE Asia and China hinterlands have persisted in sustaining their upgrading or developing their own seaports. Such a 21st century situation includes for instance Malaysia's Klang seaport and the Tanjung Pelepas seaport in the Johore state, and China's Yantian Seaport and Shekou Seaport in the Guangdong province. The underlying motivations for such seaport initiatives are alluded to nationalistic sentiments and the availability of viable profit-making seaport opportunities. Owing to the twin trends of globalization and privatization, smaller and/or newer seaports may well have better access to imported technologies and management know how, to build and operate seaports. For example,

Hong Kong's premier seaport operator, Hutchinson Seaport Holding Ltd, owns the Yantian Seaport in China and is able to bring in Hutchinson's relevant and substantial expertise. Likewise, Maersk Sealand Ltd is a terminal operator at Malaysia's Tanjung Pelepas seaport and the firm so introduced its global management systems to improve its operational efficiency.

Owing to their improved capability and desire for better returns from inward foreign and domestic investments, those smaller seaports have decided to level up their positioning from primarily feeder seaports to hub with the world's seaports network via attracting the shipping main-line services. Take the instances of Malaysia's Klang and Tanjung Pelepas seaports in which both seek to not only directly handle more of nation's cargoes, but also to aspire to turn into transhipment hubs themselves. China's newer seaports along the Pearl River Delta region are clearly positioned to cater to the growing demand of the China wide seaport services. Subsequently, China should be a less reliant hinterland for Hong Kong's seaport. Additionally, the eventual restoration of normalised trade ties between China and Taiwan should give rise to much more cargo shipment between them, while by-passing transhipment through Hong Kong. By year 2000, Shanghai started the long-term development of its Yangshan seaport, which targets 20 km of deep-water berths to handle even the largest main-line shipping vessels from Europe and North America. Shanghai's Yangshan seaport not only serves Shanghai's local economy but also as the transhipment hub for the rest of China.

The Strategic Options

Fundamental Issues

The strategic policy planning of seaport development for both Singapore and Hong Kong is a complex one. It is no longer a simple matter of projecting each of their annual economic growth rates and their associated changing seaport throughputs. Whereas Singapore and Hong Kong enjoy the head start each of having the only major transhipment seaports of Asia in the second half of the 20th century, the teeming development of regional emerging seaports have altered and sustained a new normal equilibrium for Asia's seaports moving forward. Likewise, the China wide economy has sustained robust and strong growth in the low teens over the last ten years, giving rise to sharp spikes in its imports for domestic consumption and in its manufacturing exports. Such foregoing trends offer the impetus for seaport capacity expansions to handle sharply rising nation-wide seaport throughput and maritime traffic globally.

Then, there is the question of the competition between Singapore and Hong Kong, especially for the sea borne trade routes between China and Europe. For such trade routes, can Singapore continue to play a meaningful global transhipment role, given that main line vessels can sail directly between China and Europe, without transhipment through Singapore? Confronting such a complex and competitive situational question, both the Singapore and Hong Kong seaports have to decide how they should interrogate their options for further seaport developments. Should both continue to expand seaport capacity and defend their market shares? Alternatively, should they re-orientate their option priorities, given the equally important emphasis on alternative uses of scare land, sea front, manpower and financial resources to pursue other economic development opportunities? Given that seaports are massive direct real estate complexes that consume large tracts of land, that generate significant vehicular traffic causing congestion, and that consume substantial amount of energy, due and carful considerations have to be accorded to the corresponding environmental impact and urban planning.

Model development

The conventional method of analysing policy planning for seaport throughput is the multiple regression analysis (MRA), which relies on factor estimates from historical trends. MRA's key short coming is that it is not be able to estimate the impact of new factors, which may come into play during the planning horizon. It is imperative for the policy model to enable the many factors that affect the throughput of seaports to be analysed simultaneously via a system of cause-and effect relationships. The policy model also entails provisions for multiple feedback processes that produce self-correcting or self-reinforcing responses. For example, the model is able to deal with inter related issues like how the supply of new seaport capacity influences seaport tariffs, affect shipping routes and eventually seaport throughput.

Based on the principles of system dynamics modelling, adopted in the context of political and economic systems, a 'Dynamic Seaport Performance Model (DPPM') can well be developed under the syntax of an appropriate software like "*i Think*"(Richardson 1985, Sternman 2000). The DPPM reflects not just the extrapolation of historical data but also the feedback process and the dynamic behaviour of seaport throughput vis-and-vis other political and economic factors.

Analysis and Results

The DPPM provides a comprehensive analysis of the interaction between seaport throughput and capacity expansion, with a case study on the Seaport of Hong Kong. Based on the learning derived therein, the strategic planning for the Seaport of Singapore is compared and analysed. Whilst both Hong Kong and Singapore have evolved to be amongst the worlds' busiest seaports, their trajectories of growth since the 2000s have taken somewhat divergent paths. With Hong Kong's political and economic integration with China, especially with the Pearl River Delta region, it may have somewhat devolved some of its seaport operation function thereto. Accordingly, the Hong Kong seaport throughput has stabilised at the level of about 22 mil TEU in 2014, which was only slightly more than the 18.1 mil TEU recorded in 2000. In contrast, the container throughput of the neighbouring Yantian Seaport of Shenzhen has grown from 2.1 mil TEU in 2000 to 11.7 mil in 2014. Similarly, the container throughput of the Shenzhen Seaport has grown from 4 mil TEU in 2000 to 24 mil TEU in 2014. Such throughput outcomes reveal that instead of seaport capacity expansion for Hong Kong's seaport, its growth is met by new capacity expansions of other seaports in China's Pearl River Delta, region, whilst Hong Kong's prime real estate is devoted to other uses under the discretion of its planning authority. The authority's prime consideration is to meet Hong Kong's urban development needs at that point in time.

Nevertheless, Singapore's gateway strategy has formed the fundamental basis for the growth of Singapore as an International Maritime Centre. Instead of devolution, the planning and growth of the Seaport of Singapore takes on a trajectory for step wise increase in seaport capacity expansion. Therefore, Singapore has been collaborating with shipping lines to deepen its complementary relationships with the feeder seaports. It is because the sustainable growth of seaport services demand of the feeder seaports benefits from transhipment traffic. For e.g., if the economy of Myanmar grows, more cargoes are imported to and exported from Myanmar. If the cargoes are also transhipped via Singapore then Singapore's seaport hub benefits like wise. Therefore, there exists a reinforcing loop between the feeder seaports and the seaport hub. Under such a situational scenario, the seaport hub enjoys continual economies of scale, regional and global connectivity. Accordingly, Singapore has undertaken the pathway of seaport upgrading and capacity expansion in terms of cutting-edge physical facilities and expertise in the architecture and provision of comprehensive solutions for the global maritime and logistics industry. Such architecture and provision include the offering of other seaport services like bunkering, heavy ship maintenance, ship repairs, and a wide range of ancillary services like ship management, ship brokering, ship finance, maritime law and third-party logistics services. Rather than a cost to the economy, the Seaport of Singapore is leveraged as a catalyst to generate economic multipliers, forward and backward, to reinforce the growth of the rest of the economy at large.

Sustained Seaport Development since 1971

Given the complex issue that entail economics, geo-politics and technology, it is noteworthy to look into how Singapore's seaport development has evolved over the years and what plans are afoot for the future. Prior to the arrival of the Europeans to South East Asia, Singapore's seaport had originated in the southern part of the Straits of Malacca to serve ships and traders in the region. Connectivity was made feasible with other seaports along the coast of the Malaccan Straits like Jambi, Kota Cina, Lambri, Semudra, Palembang, South Kedah and Tamiang. By the 15th century, Singapore had declined as an international trading seaport owing to the ascendance of the Malacca Sultanate. It was not until 1819 when Sir Stamford Raffles set up a trading post in Singapore and leveraged on the deep and sheltered waters at Singapore's Keppel Harbour to promote and realise maritime traffic. Over time, the Seaport of Singapore has grown along three main seaborne trade networks. The Chinese network would link Southeast Asia with the southern China seaports of Fujian and Guangdong. The Southeast Asian network would link Singapore with the islands of the Indonesian archipelago. European and Indian Ocean network would link Singapore to the markets of Europe and the South India continent. These three seaborne networks were complementary and positioned Singapore as. Therefore, Singapore grew to be the administrative capital of colonial British Malaya in the late 19th and early 20th centuries. Roads and railways were developed to transport bulky commodities like crude oil, rubber and tin from the Malay Peninsula to Singapore for processing into semi-finished products, and shipped to Britain and other international markets. During colonial rule, the transhipment hub for regional and international seaborne trade is the most important role of the Seaport of Singapore.

Since independent Singapore in 1965, the Seaport of Singapore has had to aggressively compete with other Asian seaports for regional and global seaborne trades. Singapore has so developed its export and open oriented economy via mainly value-added manufacturing. Raw and part manufactured products are sourced from regional and global markets and are subsequently exported back the raw and value-added manufactured products to such markets. Market access agreements has been readily sourced and implemented like the World Trade Organization (WTO) directives and free trade agreements. Hence, the Seaport of Singapore started from humble beginnings as Keppel Harbour, then to be later known as Keppel Terminal and eventually expanded to become today's modern and large Tanjong Pagar Terminal complex.

Container cargo handling originated in North America in the 1950s. The first shipment of containers in the world was shipped on a vessel named the 'Ideal X'. This shipping vessel carried 58 containers from Newark to Houston in 1956. In 1972, the first container ship, the M.V. Nihon, arrived in Singapore's Tanjong Pagar Terminal, owing to the foresight and vision of Mr Howe Yoon Chong, then the Chairman of the Seaport of Singapore Authority. He made the bold decision to build a container handling terminal with the loan aid from the World Bank. By 1982, the Seaport of Singapore handled 1 million TEU (ton equivalent units) for the first time. In 1990, Singapore's seaport throughput did record the high throughput mark of 5.22 million TEU. Thus, the Seaport of Singapore became the world's busiest container seaport for the first time. Hitherto, both the Keppel and Tanjong Pagar Terminals are located on mainland Singapore, fringing the Central Business District (CBD). Major seaport expansion in the 1990s added in the (Pulau i.e. island) Brani Terminal and the causeway, connecting this new Terminal to the Singapore mainland.

Nevertheless, the combination of the Keppel, Tanjong Pagar and Brani Terminals in the 1990s would only provide a total quay length of 8.4 km or 31 berths of various sizes. While the berth drafts are adequate for sizes at that point in time, provisions have to be undertaken to cater to future rising and large ship sizes, requiring deeper berth drafts. Just as the Brani Terminal comes on stream, plans are undertaken to expand the Pasir Panjang Terminal. The Pasir Panjang Terminal had been a conventional wharf and land for its expansion to be the new Pasir Panjang container terminal would require land reclamation from the sea. With the first berths of the new Pasir Panjang Terminal operational in 1998 and upon the completion of all its four phases in 2017, this new Terminal has reached its capacity throughput of about 50 million TEU per year. Additionally, the new Pasir Panjang Terminal features state of the art innovations for seaport operations like zero-pollution emission and the fully automated electric yard crane system.

The major expansion of the new Pasir Panjang Terminal is significant from the urban planning perspective. For the first time, the Seaport of Singapore would have a terminal that is not within the CBD albeit that the new Pasir Panjang Termina is a mere nearby 7 km west of the CBD. Considering that the major industrial zone of Singapore is located to the far western side of the island state at the Jurong district, almost all of the land traffic is dominated by heavy trucks and lorries, ferrying containers to and from the industrial district and Singapore's CBD seaport Terminals. To alleviate road traffic congestion, the Singapore Land Transport Authority (LTA) has built a long enough but partially elevated West Coast Highway to connect the CBD seaport terminals, and to also disperse road traffic to the Jurong industrial district.

The Future

With all the foregoing physical infrastructure provisions for the Seaport of Singapore, this Seaport has achieved a high technology and comfortable steady state for some time into the future. From the overall perspective beyond seaport physical infrastructure provisions and operations, there are considerations that make for other attractive strategic propositions. Another bigger and bolder plan is the new Tuas Seaport, first proposed by the Singapore Government's Economic Strategies Committee, 2010. The Tuas Seaport is located closer to the international seaborne trade route, offering more direct access compared with the other existing CBD seaport Terminals. In addition to being a game changer to Singapore's competitiveness in the international seaport business, the Tuas Seaport enables the relocation of the Tanjong Pagar, Keppel and Brani Terminals away from the CBD, thereby freeing up about 1,000 ha of land for urban renewal and redevelopment.

Singapore's Urban and Redevelopment Authority (URA) continues readily to share with the public, via exhibitions, seminars, dialogue sessions and publications, its design concepts that include plans to rejuvenate mainland Singapore's southern waterfront for new housing, commercial, cultural and entertainment uses. Such land uses reinforce Singapore's growing reputation as a world-class city for its people to work, live and play. The consolidation of seaport operations from the CBD seaport terminals to the Tuas district at the North Western part of the island state of Singapore, serves to minimise the need for inter-Terminal haulage by heavy trucks, lorries and vehicles. Foremost in mind is the need to resolve traffic road congestion and air pollution that contribute to significantly improving the overall built environment of Singapore, its cost effectiveness and operational efficiency.

The first set of berths at Tuas Seaport is slated to begin operations in the 2020s. When fully operational, this Tuas Seaport should be able to readily handle up to 65 million TEUs per year. Combining such a seaport throughput capacity with the 50 million TEU from the Pasir Panjang Terminal, the desired outcome is that Singapore attains the very high seaport throughput capacity of about 115 mil TEU per year. Such a desired and high throughput capacity for the Seaport of Singapore relative to its level of about 30.9 million TEU on 2015, offers Singapore more versatile headroom for the long term. Building a new terminal from scratch implies a "clean slate" to introduce more advanced technology and processes to meet future challenges. Tuas Seaport should be able to handle future generations of container ships, likely to be even larger and more complex than those ships of today. For e.g. the berths need deeper drafts to cater to the rising and large sizes of container ships like the Triple E Class, which are 400m long and have a capacity of some 20,000 TEU. These container ships tend to be thrice the size of typical container ships at the turn of the century in 2000. Correspondingly, the container quay cranes that are deployed at seaports need to be much larger to cater to the rising width and height of the ships, because the containers they hold need to be stacked up to as high as 73 meters and with 23 rows across.

For the larger container ships, as depicted in Fig 1.1, it makes economic sense for them to ply a few but key seaborne trade nodes, which connect their container cargoes to other feeder vessels at such nodes. The traditional hub and spoke strategy to enhance sea transportation efficiency should be even more attractive than before. Therefore, the evolution of the shipping industry to use larger and larger container vessels should be synergistic with Singapore's positioning as a global maritime hub. In addition, there may well be the need to cater to those ships that are powered by liquefied natural gas and other alternative fuels. Some of these technologies and processes like the automated container seaport systems, optimisation techniques, optimisation technologies and green seaport technologies, are tested under the Seaport Technology Research and Development Programme, launched by Singapore's Maritime Port Authority (MPA) and the Port of Singapore Authority (PSA) Group of Companies in April 2011.

Development of the Pasir Panjang Terminal, a former conventional seaport that is meant for non-bulky and limited handling of container cargoes, is viably feasible owing to the availability of Jurong Seaport for handling bulky cargo. Such bulky cargo includes the likes of sand, cement, bricks and granite. It is noteworthy that the former monolithic Public Works Department (PWD), subsequently scaled down to the prevailing Building Control Authority (BCA), had been working assiduously on land reclamation plans for the large scale expansion of the integrated airport and seaport complex for the Changi district, The intention has been to facilitate the versatile and sustainable viability of inter-modal operations of both sea freight and air freight cargoes. The decision is ultimately made not to go ahead with such a large physical infrastructural provision. Underpinning this critical 'walk away' decision is the key consideration that the nature of seaport services is very different from aviation services although both may well be large scale. The nature of the cargo is also very different. Aviation cargo is generally light and time sensitive. Seaport cargo is a lot heavier, containerised, pelletised or bulky in solid or liquid form. Seaport cargo tends not to be so time sensitive. As history would observe, Singapore's gateways for aviation and seaport traffic are gradually consolidated at the eastern and western tips of mainland Singapore respectively. If inter-modal transportation, inclusive of land transportation, is needed then the distance of only 50km enables such overland connectivity to be accomplished efficiently and cost effectively.

Fig 1.1. The Largest Available

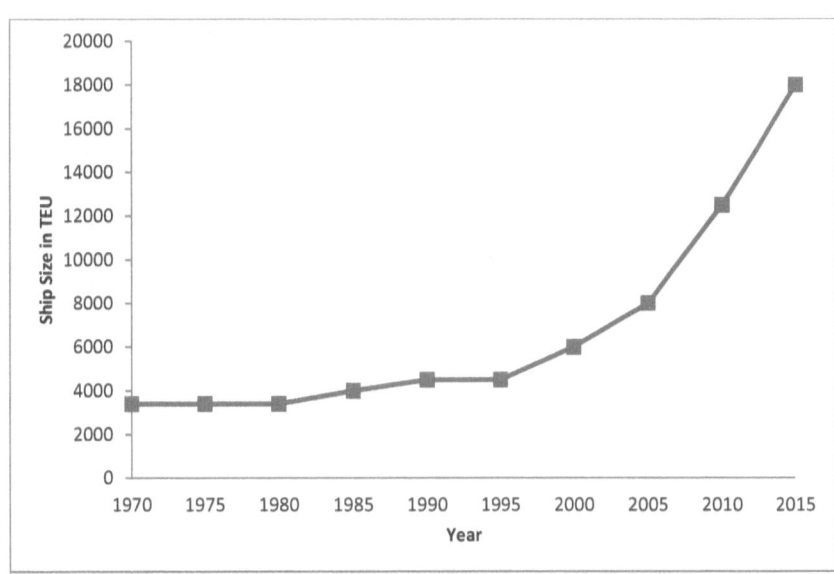

Source: Rodrigue, 2015; Authors, 2020

From Gateway To Gateway Operator

At the start, Chapter 1 examined the relationship between seaport throughput and seaport capacity expansion. Discussions leveraged on case studies of the Seaports of Singapore and Hong Kong as they share similarities but that they have chosen different strategic growth paths, appropriate for the geo-political and economic circumstances each of them faces. Given the political and economic integration between

Hong Kong and mainland China, Hong Kong has devolved some of its previous seaport roles to the newer China seaports, particularly those seaports in the Pearl River Delta. While Singapore has continued to invest in and deploy newer and larger terminals equipped with the state-of-the-art technology, to further develop not only the Seaport of Singapore but to transform Singapore into an 'International Maritime Hub', which is complemented by the comprehensive eco-system of logistics, shipping, finance and legal services.

Closely associated with the large and complex physical and maritime infrastructural provisions of the Seaport of Singapore, the corporate form of the organization that own and run the Seaport of Singapore has in turn evolved. Prior to 1993, such a corporate organisation assumed the form of a government statutory body, the Port of Singapore Authority (PSA), under the purview of Singapore's Ministry of Transport and Communications. Since 1993, PSA was devolved to become the corporatized PSA International Ltd. Beyond operating the Seaport of Singapore, PSA International Ltd is also the owner and terminal operator in many parts of the world. As at 2015, the global footprint of PSA International Ltd has included the seaports of Belgium, China, Columbia, Italy, India, Indonesia, Japan, Korea, Pakistan, 'Sea Portugal', Saudi Arabia, Thailand, Turkey and Vietnam. By 2014, the global container throughput of PSA International has reached some 65.44 million TEU, including some 33.6 mil TEU from the Seaport of Singapore. In other words, half of PSA International Ltd.'s throughput is derived from abroad. Therefore, PSA International Ltd and its 30 seaports both in Singapore and in the rest of the world is more than capable to offer, from its network of seaports, comprehensive services at the global level to the likes of shipping lines, third party logistic-services providers, to shippers and consignees.

For the myriad set of activities and comprehensive services at the global level, there has to be a body that can take the lead in planning and co-ordinating the strategic stewardship for long term growth of Singapore's maritime industry. Prior to 1996, such a role for strategic stewardship was consolidated within the Post of Singapore Authority (PSA), a large and complex government statutory board.

Nevertheless, and in 1996, the Maritime and Port Authority (MPA) was constituted to take on the crucial and multiple roles of seaport regulator, seaport planner and of the leading global 'think tank', which serves the interest of the global maritime community. In this regard, the MPA has set up and run its own 'MPA Academy'. This Academy has introduced and stepped up various initiatives for seaport and maritime research and development (R & D). The MPA therefore plays a pivotal role in providing the stewardship to develop Singapore as the premier global seaport hub and as the international maritime centre (IMC), to advance and safeguard Singapore's strategic maritime interests.

An Institutional Policy Framework

In addition, it is hoped that Chapter 1 offers planners, policy makers and investors a structured framework of analysis to look into possible questions and the appropriate policies on seaport and maritime matters of global interest. Going forward, the key concerns include the global network of seaports associated with Singapore, and the wider context of Singapore's relationship with the global maritime community as an international maritime centre. As Singapore continues to grow sustainably, there is likely to be pressure to limit further allocation of land for seaport and airport developments in favour of other higher yielding commercial and industrial real estate uses.

In other words, the approach taken by Hong Kong earlier in partially externalising its seaport services may become an attractive proposition for Singapore in the future, especially if such a proposition is analysed purely from the economic and financial perspectives, vis-à-vis the land premium that the government can command between zoning the land for commercial/industrial or for seaport uses. However, further discussion entails fundamental strategic rethinking, which should not be analysed purely with economic and financial considerations alone. Indeed, the ascendance of the Trans-Pacific

Partnership (TPP) as well as the formation of the ASEAN Economic Community (AEC) will likely bring about increased trade flow between Asia and the Americas as well as within South East Asia. There is bound to be considerable upside potential to maritime throughput for the Seaport of Singapore as well as carriers that uses Singapore as the hub.

Supply Chain Management (SCM)

In the early days, cargo handling involved primarily the transportation of goods. Accordingly, at the seaports, you can find only ships, cranes, some forklifts, and storage yards in some warehouses or open space. As discussed earlier, cargo handling has evolved to become a lot more complex that require elegant solutions that can only be put together with specialised knowledge. Such specialised knowledge is encompassed within a concept of supply chain management (SCM). A working group on logistics of the Economic Review Committee commissioned by the Singapore government has recommended that Singapore should be developed into a global integrated logistics hub, i.e. global gateway. The discussion in this section highlights the key aspects of this recommendation and elaborate on a few aspects that are useful for translating the strategic intentions to implementation terms.

Beyond transportation and cargo handling *per se*, SCM is a concept that incorporates components of services within the entire logistics value chain to offer customers a complete "end-to-end" service from suppliers to end customers. Accordingly, instead of the shippers or consignees having to source and decide how the cargoes are to be transported, which shipping or airlines to use, which seaport or airport to go to, as well as various other details, they appoint operators in the SCM to handle all these for them. In recognition of the specialist knowledge required, there is a global trend of increasing preference by companies to opt for integrative SCM outsourcing models. It is inevitable to entail the co-ordination and transfer of three flows, i.e. the cargoes themselves, the associated information that communicate the nature of the cargoes and where they may be at any one point in time, and the funds required to be paid to the different service providers in the value chain to effect the movements and transfers. Please see Fig. 1.2.

Fig 1.2. Components of Supply Chain Management (SCM)

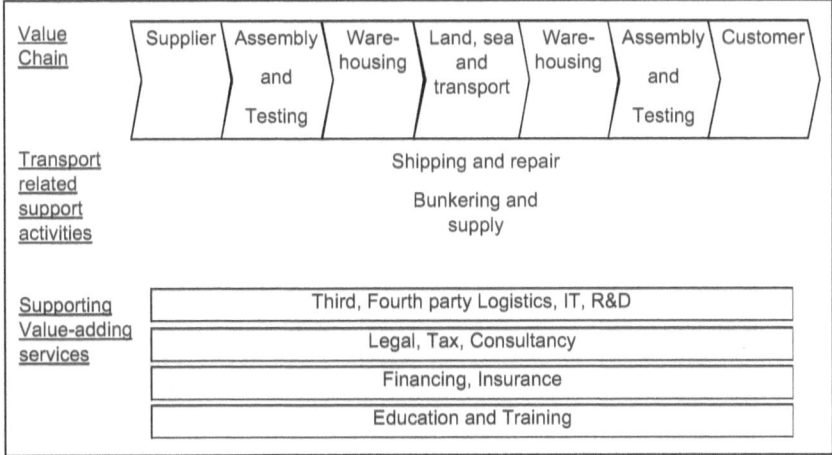

Source: ERC, 2012; Authors, 2020.

ERC (2002) estimated that the global SCM market would have grown to US$173.7 billion by 2005. This would have represented a compound annual growth rate (CAGR) of 10% of the preceding three years. Specifically, the Asian SCM market is poised for robust growth. Annual SCM growth rates are projected at 7% in Europe, 10% in North America, and 15% in Asia, as indicated by a JP Morgan Research survey. In this survey, Asian shippers are found to have outsourced only about 2.5% of their logistics functions as compared to between 20%-25% by their US and European counterparts, thus indicating substantial headroom and opportunities for growth. Accordingly, Singapore, riding on a strong foundation of having a good port has recognised the long term continual development of the Port of Singapore cannot be just focused on the port *per se*. It will have to tie in with developing its logistics sector within a supply chain management framework.

However, Singapore is not the only country try to do this. But each country will have their unique strength that allow them to do certain things better than the others. Prior to implanting such a plan, it will be necessary to examine with more details about the Strength, Weaknesses, Opportunities and Threats (SWOT) of Singapore's transport and logistics industry. This is shown in Table 1.1.

Table 1: SWOT Analysis Of Singapore's Transport & Logistics Industry (Source: Adapted From

Strength	Weaknesses
- Strong physical infrastructure, with potential to make them better. - Good connectivity to major trading and manufacturing bases by air and sea. - Major shippers and logistics service providers have their regional headquarters and offices in Singapore. - Stable political, economic and social conditions. - An educated workforce. - A strong legal system and business friendly tax structure. - Pro-active government support for bilateral and multi-lateral initiatives.	- Relatively high costs, especially land rentals and wages. - Limited land and domestic market. - Industry is fragmented, lacks scale, and not integrated. - Instances of lack of a logistics cluster / ecosystem. - Lack of responsiveness to customers' needs. - Shortage of skilled and experienced workforce who are also entrepreneurial. - Inadequate technological capabilities to carry out large scale activities. - Weak marketing of Singapore as a logistics/supply chain hub.
Opportunities	Threats
- Strong growth potential for logistics outsourcing in Asia. - Potential to synergy with offshore trade conducted by Singapore based companies. - Positive reputation of Singapore as a secure logistics hub. - Introduction of mega ships that will favour the hub and stoke approach.	- Relocation of manufacturing and distribution bases to other regional hubs (e.g. China). - Competitions from other governments employing the same strategies. - Preference of direct route over the hub-and spoke approach which may reduce the traffic through Singapore.

Source: ERC, 2012; Authors, 2020.

From the SWOT analysis of Table 1,1, the strategic plan for the developing the SCM industry is formulated. The underlying foundation is encapsulated in the overall 'Vision for Singapore' in this regard as follows:

> "To develop Singapore into a leading global integrated logistics hub, with robust maritime, aviation, and land transport capabilities supporting the global economy" (Source: ERC, 2012).

Based on such a Vision, the strategic plan can be drilled down into the development of the specific sub-sectors, as illustrated in Fig 1.3.

Fig 1.3. Components of the Supply Chain Management (SCM)

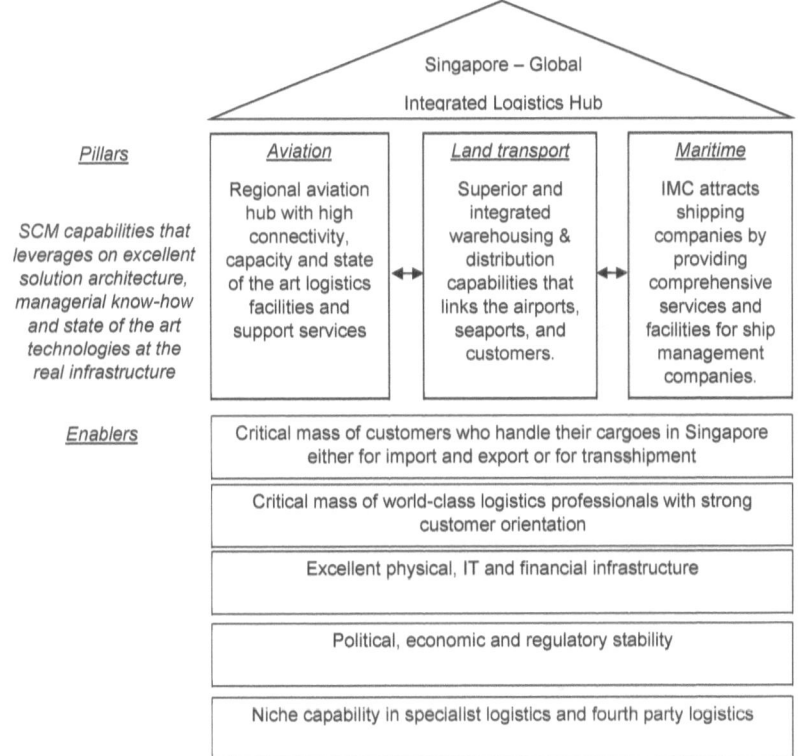

Source: ERC, 2012; Authors, 2020

As expounded in the vision and depicted in Fig 1.3, the overall aim is to develop Singapore as a 'Global Integrated Logistics Hub'. It such a logistic hub, companies in Singapore function as the nerve centre to control and manage activities and assets of global supply chains across an expanded hinterland (Konings, 1996). But such SCM activities cannot be undertaken for their own sake. They have to be built upon real infrastructures and the associated services. In other words, while the over-arching strategic intention is to drive the growth of the SCM sector, the operationalization entails the spearheading of the growth of the maritime, aviation, and land transport sectors as pillars of growth.

a. Maritime: This entails Singapore becoming an international maritime centre (IMC) by attracting shipping companies to use Singapore as the transhipment hub. Correspondingly, such shipping companies will also need to be served by services for bunkering, ship management, ship repairs etc. Thus, the IMC positioning should also seek to attract these other companies to locate in Singapore.

b. Aviation: This entails Singapore becoming a regional aviation hub with high connectivity and capacity, and state-of-the-art logistics and support facilities. Chapter 4 will discuss the details of this, which would encompass further drilling down to the development of specific programmes for passenger and cargo services, as well as aviation and aerospace industry.

c. Land Transport: Cargo handling at the gateways in Singapore needs to be supported by warehousing and local land transportation. Specifically, these are for supporting the consolidation and distribution activities, which may also include inter-modal operations.

Whilst the above three pillars can be considered as the strategic business thrusts, their growths are subjected to the availability of conducive environment and supporting soft infrastructures, such as the following:

a. Stability and predictability in the political, economic and regulatory environment. This has been a long-standing guiding philosophy of Singapore. Such an environment will be favourable to business. Over the years, the track record of Singapore in this regard has been its tower of strength. It should continue to defend this as a key value-add to the international business community (Lee, 2015).
b. Excellent physical, IT, and financial infrastructure. Singapore's long-term and sustained commitments in these regards are explicitly articulated in the development concept Plan, IT master plan, and various programmes of the ministries in charge of national development, IT, as well as the finance and monetary policies.
c. Critical mass of logistics professionals with strong customer orientation. This critical mass requires the provision of courses at the local institutions of higher learning for the training of such professionals and post-graduation continuous professional development. As logistics is invariably a globalised business, Singapore should also be welcoming to attract talents from the other parts of the world who can augment the local talents and bring with them global network and connections for business development purposes.
d. Niche capabilities. The demand for transport has evolved from a demand for the transfer of goods to an integrated demand for the transfer of goods and the associated information that have been added value, timely, reliably and cost-efficiently (Panayides, 2006). Indeed, while container cargo handling and third-party logistics services have become a somewhat commoditised capability where most ports and service providers in various parts of the world are able offer, the ability to offer specialist logistic services such as that for project cargoes, equipment for the oil and gas industry, hazardous cargoes, high value and high security cargoes or those that are highly time sensitive have remained confined to a limited pool of experts, who accordingly are able to levy

a premium for their services (Hertz, Susanne, and Alfredsson, 2003). As such and instead of doing more of the same, in terms of generic airport and seaport operations and third party logistics services, specialist logistics and fourth party logistics services are more sustainable niche for Singapore who cannot continue to compete with price and scale alone.

e. Critical mass of customers who handle their cargoes in Singapore either for import and export or for transhipment. This will entail developing the Singapore economy as a whole. The growth of the manufacturing sector results in more cargoes to be handled directly. The growth of the Singapore economy in general leads to higher standard of living amongst the local population, which in turn require the import of more goods to support local consumption.

ERC (2012) also calls for measures to reduce the land costs for seaport and airport operations. Whilst this is welcoming for the operators of these facilities, further analysis needs to be considered from the overall considerations of the opportunity costs of the land reclaimed at high costs to be set aside for these uses as against other potential uses. Secondly, the externality that is derived from such infrastructure development and operations should be examined so that the land price can be determined with rationale computations, founded on economic principles (Williams, A. W., 1991). The quest to lower costs should also be directed at efforts to innovate and to deploy appropriate technologies for improving land and labour productivity, the two key resources that are needed but are aspects that Singapore faces severe constraints. Much progress has been made hitherto, be it in terms of design of seaports, the deployment of automation in various stages of cargo handling, or the exploitation of contemporary IT solutions for operational controls or business analytics. It is however noted that in the final analysis, the decisions are not answers to some economic questions. They should be guided by the strategic considerations of the overall competitiveness of Singapore.

Key References

Button, Kenneth. Transport economics. Edward Elgar Publishing, 2010.

ERC Working Group on Logistics (2012). Developing Singapore into a global integrated logistics hub. International Enterprise Singapore.

Hertz, Susanne, and Monica Alfredsson. "Strategic development of third party logistics providers." Industrial marketing management 32, no. 2 (2003): 139-149.

Konings, J. W. "Integrated centres for the transhipment, storage, collection and distribution of goods: A survey of the possibilities for a high-quality intermodal transport concept." Transport Policy 3, no. 1 (1996): 3-11.

Lee, H. L. "Singapore: Long-term vision is to become a global city". Global. http://www.global-briefing.org. Access 22 January 2015.

Panayides, Photis M. "Maritime logistics and global supply chains: towards a research agenda." Maritime Economics & Logistics 8, no. 1 (2006): 3-18.

Williams, Alan W. "A guide to valuing transport externalities by hedonic means." Transport Reviews 11, no. 4 (1991): 311-324.

Van Klink, H. Arjen, and Geerke C. van Den Berg. "Gateways and intermodalism." Journal of transport geography 6, no. 1 (1998): 1-9.

CHAPTER 2

RISK MANAGEMENT IN LARGE PHYSICAL INFRASTRUCTURE INVESTMENT: THE CONTEXT OF SEAPORT INFRASTRUCTURE DEVELOPMENT AND INVESTMENT

Singapore companies have been venturing abroad to generate growth while in the emerging East Asian economies that are attracting green field developments, the existing physical infrastructure of Asian economies is still rudimentary. In many instances, the development of basic physical infrastructure becomes a pre-requisite, as it is needed to underpin other types of direct real estate by making such direct real estate suitable for occupation (see Fig 2.1). The basic physical infrastructure has to even compete with other types of direct real estate investment for funding. It is thus important to enhance one's understanding of the risk-return characteristics of investments in large physical infrastructure projects, so that investors find them attractive. Banks can also better appraise them accordingly.

Fig 2.1. Different types of real estate investments

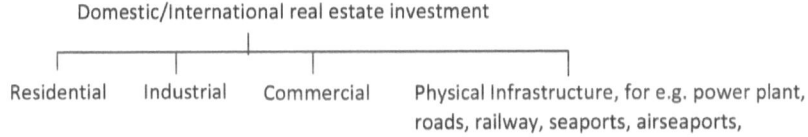

Source: Authors, 2020

While Chapter 2 may focus on best practices on investment appraisal and risk management, such a subject matter tends to be commercially sensitive (Simister, 1994). Investment decisions may even well be based on the personal judgement of business owners, and hence not rigorously documented. Therefore, cross-sectional and focus group studies tend to concentrate on few and selected variables, and on certain subsystems. Under these circumstances, the acquisition of limited data precludes in-depth analysis, or even worse, leads to incomplete or distorted assessments (Roberts and Rouseau, 1989). Owing to the "specificity" of large-scale projects, any normalisation or comparison between different projects and different companies is bound to be difficult. If at all possible, a large sample size is required to enable meaningful categorisation and comparisons (Ho *et. al.*, 1992). Therefore, a case-based approach that involves the empirical examination of a particular phenomenon, utilizing multiple sources of evidence, may well be appropriate. The Jurong Seaport, which is the only industrial seaport in the island-state of Singapore, is taken to be the context for the case study.

As a result, the main objective of Chapter 2 is to examine a rigorous framework for risk management in infrastructural projects, using the seaport as the case example. This is relevant as seaport investments are large and complex, and their success or failures will have long-term implications. As the seaport impacts the economic development of the hinterland it serves, and vice versa, the seaport's success will not only be of interest to investors but also to governments, owing to externalities spilling over into the hinterland's economy.

The paper is organised into several sections. The first section provides the introduction while the next (second) section looks at the related literature. Various new concepts are also discussed, namely, the public good nature of physical infrastructure and the theoretical conceptions of risk and risk management within the project feasibility context. The third section discusses the theoretical framework of analysis for Chapter 2. The fourth section discusses the risk simulation and model estimations while the fifth section concludes the Chapter's findings.

The Related Literature

Physical Infrastructure as a Public Good

The term "infrastructure" evolved during the Second World War by military strategists to reflect the elements of warfare logistics. Economists had introduced the term on the literature of development economics, to be used interchangeably with "overhead capital" (Youngson, 1967). The 1950s and the 1960s did witness a surge of developmental economic studies in order to further classify physical infrastructure. Lewis (1955) includes public utilities and seaports in such a classification. Higgins (1959) includes transseaport, public utilities, schools and hospitals. Hirschman (1958) lists law and order, education, public health, transpotation, communications, power, water, irrigation, and drainage. The subsequent consensus is that the creation of physical infrastructure requires public initiatives, and it provides the basic environment to support the productive activities of individuals as well as groups in society. Such consensus represents the classical view of physical infrastructure as a public good, which is created to generate further external economies (technological and pecuniary) and social benefits. In this sense, the collateral on a seaport project is not confined to only direct seaport income but also to any subsequent national and regional development, such as the expansion of gross domestic product, employment creation and the raising of national and regional tax revenues.

SEAPORT AND AIRPORT INFRASTRUCTURE ECONOMICS AND POLICY - A SINGAPORE PERSPECTIVE

Econometric models have been developed in order to quantify the contribution of seaports to the public good (Ho, 1994). These models examine the historical trends of relevant variables and relate them through estimated, mathematical, functional forms. However, owing to their complexity, these models are not widely used in industry.

Fig 2.2. A Seaport's Key Activities in Reality

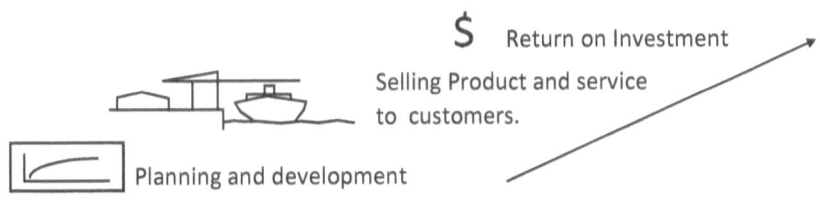

Source: Authors, 2020

Contrary to the classical view of seaports as public infrastructure, seaports can in reality be planned, developed and operated in the anticipation of market demand, as depicted in Fig 2.2, while achieving an expected risk-adjusted return under the principle of commercial profit (Seafarer, 1995). Thus, investment risk management strategies can be developed with respect to their special characteristics. Ahmed et. al. (1992), Rosenstein-Rodan (1943), Nurske (1953), and Plymton and Brunker (1992) have established that infrastructural investments are typically large and capital intensive, requiring long gestation periods, and are location specific. Unlike housing development where the payback period is short, and as the development is generally conducted as a "Built-and-Transfer" investment strategy, the infrastructural project requires a long-term payback period as it is generally conducted as a "Built-Operate-and-Transfer" investment strategy. Furthermore, seaport projects tend to be indivisible or 'lumpy" investments, implying that they are subject to long periods of excess capacity.

As a consequence, investors require higher rates of return that are risk adjusted (Plymton and Brunke, 1992). There has been an emerging trend in the successful privatisation of infrastructural and seaport projects, signifying that despite the higher risks involved, private investments in physical infrastructure can be viable and sustainable strategic opportunities (PA, 1992). Correspondingly, favourable regulatory environments have significantly contributed to the dilution of risks, which are borne by the private sector.

Risk Conceptions

Hargitay and Yu (1993) define investments as activities that require cash outlay (i.e. investment capital) with the aim of receiving, in return, future cash inflow. As no one can predict the future, risks and uncertainty are therefore part and parcel of all investments. While uncertainty alone may not be threatening, it is the resulting impact of the uncertain event that is important (Ho *et. al.*, 1992). Hertz *et. al.* (1984) attribute the origin of risk and uncertainty to the lack of predictability about problem structure, outcomes or consequences. Most methodologies expound the treatment of risks and uncertainty to rely on some form of modelling of the perceived real world, and the extrapolation based on past trends. Since models are of necessity simplifications of reality, where continuous variables have been made discrete, an infinite number of mathematical expressions or processes has been made finite or truncated (Funtowicz *et. al.*, 1990).

However, forecasts derived from these foregoing models often have limited empirical validity (Peters, 1991). Arlt (1986) highlights that forecasting can be used to reduce the area over which judgement has to be exercised, so that thought processes can be focused. Clark (1990) argues that forecasting also support contingency planning, which allows prompt, controlled and pre-evaluated responses to be implemented, should risks materialise. Thus, whilst risk management does not eliminate risks, it brings us closer to the predictions that nonetheless are an improvement on un-directed guesses. In practice, risk management can structure projects in order to optimise risks so that companies, which participate in risk-taking, can do so deliberately and with the opportunity to acquire maximum benefit, while facing a limited and controlled exposure.

Risk management can be broadly divided into risk identification, risk analysis and risk control, as depicted in Fig 2.3. Risk identification is the explicit recognition of the difficulties and the critical implementation factors, which can cause project failures (Mustafa *et. al.*, 1991). The risks identified can also be classified according to the various sources of uncertainty, such as data uncertainties (quality and reliability of data), modelling uncertainties (i.e. incomplete understanding of the modelled phenomena or error from mathematical approximations) and completeness uncertainty (the lack of complete knowledge and are by definition unquantifiable and irreducible) (Funtowicz *et. al.*, 1990).

Fig 2.3. Key Aspects of Risk Management

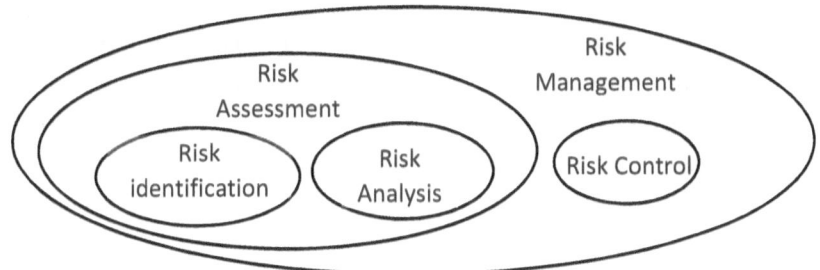

Source: Ho *et. al.*, 1992

Subsequent to risk identification, risk analysis can be conducted to quantify risks that can be expressed in statistical forms on the assumption that risk is purely a technical issue, and can be resolved within the framework of mathematical equations. The process of inputting ranges and probabilities to selected risky variables makes explicit what is implicit in many qualitative appraisals (Jones, 1991). Any inconsistency in qualitative appraisal can also be ferreted out.

Risk analysis is most advanced in the construction, finance, nuclear, aerospace, and defence industries where the consequence of failure can be catastrophic (Roberts and Rousseau, 1989; Kobylarz, 1992; Chris Chapman, 1987; Jones, 1991). Common tools of risk analysis include the Delphi method, Monte Carlo simulations, the

Process Evaluation and Review Technique (PERT), Controlled Interval and Memory Modelling (CIM), Analytic Hierarchy Process (Mustafa and Al-Bahar, 1991), the Integrated Model for Decision and Risk Management (IMDRiM) (Ho, *et. al.*, 1992), scenario planning, game theory, utility theory, systems thinking (Checkland and Scholes, 1990), organisation behaviours (Roberts and Rousseau, 1990), and newer techniques like the catastrophic theory, fuzzy-set theory or multi-criteria decision-making models. However, it must be emphasized that there is no correlation between technique sophistication and risk management effectiveness.

Risk control is aimed at containing the threats of the risks so that the chances of their occurrences and the associated impacts, fall within reasonable limits. Strategies that can be adopted include those to remove, reduce, avoid, and transfer risks (Clark, *et. al.* 1990). In addition, the partial transfer of risks to other parties, or risk sharing as in joint ventures, can also be undertaken. Plymton and Brunke (1992) rationalize that the aim is to achieve a trade-off so that there is some equilibrium position, whereby enough risk is distributed to induce activity but not enough to fundamentally alter the incentives for productive activity.

Risk Management in Large Project Feasibility Study

Clark *et. al.* (1990) define a feasibility project to be a non-repetitive undertaking in order to produce a defined outcome along the predetermined path and period. The risk dimensions in project management are different from those for functional management, which deals mainly with familiar, repetitive work in an operating environment that is relatively stable (Scotto, 1994). Typically, the lifecycle of large direct real estate projects consists of several key stages:

- concept formulation;
- feasibility study;
- preliminary design;

- sanction;
- tendering; and
- execution.

As the large direct real estate project progresses from one phase to another, different environmental forces act upon it, and different risk management responses are required to contain them at the least (as depicted in Fig 2.4). The emphasis should be on risk identification at the initial stages of the project so that risk models can be developed to support the analysis of such risks. Based on such an analysis, risk control mechanisms can be structured in order to optimize risk exposure. When a large project is finally implemented, risk control activities will be stepped up (Clark *et. al.*, 1990).

Fig 2.4. Changing Focus of Risk Management During the Life Cycle of a Large Project

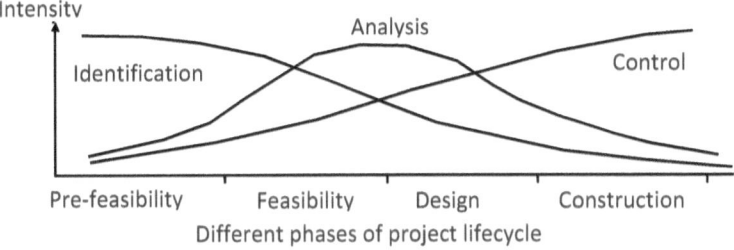

Source: Authors, 2020

In a feasibility study that takes on the risk dimension, input parameters such as interest rates and market size are stochastically treated as probability distributions, rather than as discreet numbers (Hull, 1990). In Fig 2.5, only single point estimates are given for two project proposals. They contain no measure of quality and they belie the existence of a range of possible outcomes.

On this basis, Project B seems to offer a higher return on the investment. In Fig 2.6, estimates are expressed as probability distributions to reflect the uncertainty surrounding the outcomes of each proposal. It shows that although the outcome of Project B can be higher than Project A, the variability, and thus the risk, of this outcome is also higher. On the other hand, Project A offers a lower return, but the chances of its return falling short of expectation is rather small. In other words, Project A may well be the superior choice given the uncertainties surrounding Project B.

Fig 2.5. Single point estimates provided by traditional decision process.

Fig 2.6. Estimates with uncertainty which are reflected in probability density functions.

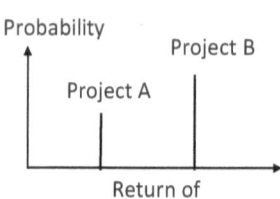

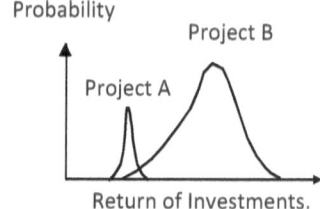

Source: Authors, 2020

The Theoretical Framework of Analysis

Fig. 2,7 depicts the theoretical framework of analysis for Chapter 2. It is formulated on the fundamental philosophy that Singapore's Jurong Port seeks to create its privately desired environment, and to provide the physical facilities that are desired by its customers so that they can collaborate with the Jurong Port, in order to establish their international linkages as well as to expand their businesses. On this basis, a comprehensive review of the competitive environment, internal and external, is initially made. Thereafter, the development potential and the various strategic choices for Jurong Port are examined vis-à-vis the market opportunities.

Planned scenarios under scenario planning and feasibility analyses under structured Monte-Carlo risk simulation modelling are to be conducted, while constraint programming techniques can be examined to address the uncertainties associated in the process of evaluating the development potential.

Infrastructural Investment Strategy

There are only two seaports in Singapore – the PSA (Port of Singapore) Corporation is primarily a container seaport and has been the world's second busiest container seaport after Hong Kong in 1995, handling around 12 million TEUs (twenty feet equivalent units). Almost 80% of PSA's throughput is for transhipment, mainly to Malaysia, Thailand and Indonesia. The other seaport is the Jurong Port, set up in 1963 to complement PSA Corporation, to facilitate the import of raw materials to the vast Jurong Industrial Estate at the western end of the island-state of Singapore (with Jurong Port handling about 12.3 million tonnes of cargo in the historical period between April 1995 and March 1996). PSA had the early head start and much benefitted from the first mover advantage, and by end 2004 PSA handled more than 20 million TEU. In contrast, PSA is a regional hub serving much more than Malaysia, Thailand and Indonesia, and PSA is also the cargo consolidation hub for Europe and the Americas.

Fig 2.7. The Theoretical Framework of Analysis

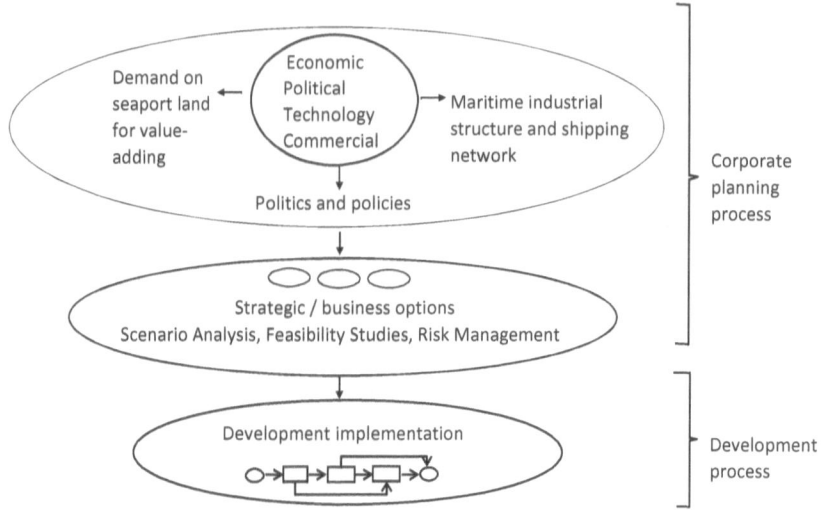

Source: Authors, 2020

Fig. 2.8. Total Sea Cargo Handled by the Seaport of Singapore (PSA Corp)

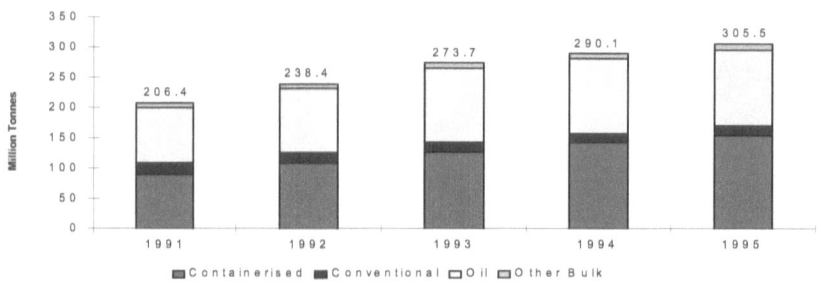

Source: PSA Corp., Selected Annual Reports; Authors, 2020

The market-segment mix of Jurong Seaport can be broadly divided into two categories: "Cargo Related" (i.e. berthing of vessels, loading and unloading cargo), and "Real Asset Related" (i.e. leasing of warehouses, open storage yard, land, etc.). These two business categories are mutually supportive. The former generates demand for warehouses and storage yards. The latter, like the long-term land leases for seaport-related industries (for e.g. cement terminals, lube oil plants, etc.), which generates inelastic derived demand for cargo through the berths. General cargo handled in Jurong Seaport is of the conventional form, i.e. non-containerised cargo. This includes vehicles, steel products, and project cargoes such as machinery, cars, mining vehicles, military hardware, etc. It is clear even from the early historical trend of Fig 2.8 that Jurong port excelled in its specialisation of bulky-cargo handling. From historical records, like that of Table 2.1 in the early days of 1992 to 1996, Jurong Port did outpace PSA Corp to reach about 40% share of the market of conventional cargo traffic in Singapore.

It is noteworthy that Jurong Port does not handle many containers due to its lacking of container-handling infrastructure. There is however, a standing and informal arrangement whereby PSA Corporation focusses on container handling while Jurong Port only handles bulk and limited conventional cargo. Nevertheless, Jurong port's specialisation of bulky-cargo handling is subject to directional policy at the discretion of Singapore's Ministry of Transport and Communications.

Table 2.1. Early Conventional Cargo Traffic Trend In Singapore

Financial year	91/92	92/93	93/94	94/95	95/96
PSA Corp	13.1	11.9	10.5	9.1	9.0
Jurong Port (JP)	4.0	4.6	5.3	5.5	6.4
Total	17.1	16.5	15.8	14.6	15.4
JP's market share	23%	28%	34%	38%	42%

NB. Values are in million tonnes.
Source: Selected statistical reports, PSA Corp and Jurong Seaport; Authors, 2020

Bulk cargo at the Jurong Seaport mainly comprises cement, clinker, copper slag, sugar, lube oil, vegetable oil and dry chemicals. From Table 2.2 almost all are imports even in the early years (up to about 5.9 million tonnes in total by 1996). As these are dependent on Singapore's open economy in the steady state, the bulk cargo growth is virtually not anticipated while potential new bulk transhipment, if at all, is to be of the customised type that requires specialised handling and storage systems. The existing bulky-cargo handling system is aging, at least 25 years old[1], and that the system has to be substantially upgraded because the existing sytem is not able to sustain the relatively high throughput of 20 million tonnes of sand and aggregates, via barges in the 3,000 dwt capacity-class.

Table 2.2. Steady State Throughput Performance
(Historical FY91/92 To FY95/96 Data)

Type of Cargo	FY 91/92	FY 92/93	FY 93/94	FY 94/95	FY 95/96
Bulk					
Cement Clinker	1.76	2.02	2.53	2.37	3.34
Bulk Fertilizer	1.77	0.19	0.14	0.11	0.07
Dry Chemical	0.24	0.22	0.25	0.24	0.29
Raw Sugar	0.17	0.15	0.15	0.17	0.20
Bulk Grain	0.22	0.15	0.16	0.04	0.03
Copper Slag	0.44	0.42	0.33	0.34	0.39
Scrap Iron	0.18	0.20	0.43	0.24	0.33
Liquid Bulk	0.42	0.40	0.41	0.87	0.90
Others (Bulk)	0.37	0.42	0.42	0.32	0.30
Total bulk	3.98	4.17	4.81	4.71	**5.86**
Conventional					
Bag Fertilizer	0.1	0.11	0.04	0.03	0
Bulk Grain	0	0	0.02	0.02	0
Frozen Fish	0.05	0.03	0.02	0.04	0.04
Others (General)	1.87	2.08	2.43	2.65	2.83
Neo-bulk					
Steel Products	1.74	2.06	2.61	2.57	3.29
Logs/Timber	0.23	0.29	0.23	0.22	0.23
Total conventional	3.99	4.57	5.35	5.53	6.39
Grand total	7.97	8.75	10.15	10.24	12.27

---

[1] Such cranes handle only 6-7 tonnes per grab or 120 tonnes/hr. Productivity of modern cranes can reach magnitudes in excess of 20 tonnes per grab or 400 tonnes per hour.

| Conventional cargo/ total throughput. | 50% | 64% | 53% | 54% | 52% |

All numbers in million tonnes. Source: Selected Statistical Reports of Jurong Seaport; Authors, 2020

Jurong Port's other key line of business is the leasing of land and warehouses. This line of business has not been fully realized as evident from the generally low occupancy of land, subject to an overall low plot ratio of 0.2. Table 2.3 shows that land constitutes nearly three quarters of the market value of Jurong Seaport's total assets, followed by the berths and warehouses. Inspection of available and permitted plans suggests that by around mid-2000s say end 2006, a third of the existing 120 ha of the free trade zone land FTZ land, and about two thirds of the 90 ha of the non-FTZ land, can be set aside for seaport related industries and logistics services.

Table 2.3. Total Asset Value of ghe Jurong Port

Type	Size	Replacement cost (RC)	'RC' % of physical assets
Land area (total)	220 ha	$1.74 bil[2]	73%
Land area (Free Trade Zone)	120 ha	$0.95 bil	
Warehouse & ancillary buildings	160,000 sqm	$96 mil[3]	4%
Berths	4,400m	$530 mil[4]	23%
Total		**$2.37 bil**	**100%**

Source: Selected Statistical Reports of Jurong Seaport; Authors, 2020

[2] The estimate on replacement cost is based on S$792/sqm for 99 year leasehold (i.e. S$792/sqm * 220 ha = S$1.74 bil). The total area includes general infrastructure like reserves for road and public utilities. Replacement cost is with new and latest technology. Land area is optimally safeguarded via dialogue and consensus among port engineering and land surveying considerations in combination with urban planning stipulations.

[3] Based on unit construction of S$6,000/sqm.

[4] Based on construction cost of S$120,000 per metre run for berths, including the related yard area.

Analysis of Financial Performance in Brief

Jurong Port's revenue fluctuates in line with Singapore's economic cycle - declining from S$42.3 million in the early 1980s to S$23.3 million in the late 1980s, owing to an economic recession and the corresponding downward revision of seaport tariffs. As a consequence of the broad-based economic recovery in the early 1990s, Jurong Port's revenue has expanded at a high average annual rate of 13 % p.a. to a record high of S$72.8 million by the mid-1990s. Revenue then grows at a faster rate than port throughput, indicating that revenue growth originates more from seaport tariff hikes rather than from seaport throughput growth. The implication is that Jurong Port's revenue sources are very much dependent on its traditional markets and their associated risks.

Jurong Port's corresponding expenditure significantly drops by 16 % from about S$19.66 million in the early 1980s to about S$16.5 million by mid-1980s, owing to a scaling-down of operations in the years of economic recession. Thereafter, expenditure expands robustly at 8.9 % p.a. to a high of S$35.6 million by mid-1990s, as observed in Table 2.4. The slower expenditure growth relative to revenue growth is largely due to the reduction in depreciation expenses (arising from the aging of cargo handling equipment) over the same period. Operating surplus ratio (i.e. the surplus before contribution to the government's consolidation fund over the gross income) is found to fall from the ratio of 0.54 in the early 1980s to a low of 0.29 by the mid-1980s, before expectedly recovering to a sustainable ratio of 0.44 by the mid-1990s and well through to the 2020s.

The return on assets (ROA) is based on the historical cost of land via residual land valuation. If the market rent is imputed at S$44.6 per sqm per year, the prevailing rate at which Jurong Port charges its customers, then the ROA can trough unappealingly to as low as -4.8% in FY 1995/1996, as shown in Table 2.5. The Table is also indicative of further opportunities for the still productive assets of Jurong Port to exploit to enable its ROA to rebound optimally from the low base effect.

Table 2.4. Income, Expenditure And Surplus

	Financial year *(All values in S$ million)*				
	91/92	92/93	93/94	94/95	95/96
Income	47.3	54.3	58.5	59.4	72.8
Expenditure	24.8	24.1	30.0	32.8	35.6
Surplus before consol fund	19.4	24.9	21.6	21.0	31.9
Surplus after consol fund	15.5	19.9	17.2	16.8	25.5
Fixed assets (net book value) ($)	271	325	339	338	376
Return on Assets	5.7%	6.1%	5.1%	5.0%	7.9%

Source: Selected Statistical Reports of Jurong Seaport; Authors, 2020

Table 2.5. Financial Performance For FY 95/96 With Imputed Market Land Rent

Expenditure (excl land rent)	S$ 35.6 mil
Land rent @ S$44.6/sqm/yr * 120 ha	S$ 53.5 mil
Surplus before consol fund	S$ - 16.3mil
Fixed assets (net book value)	S$ 343 mil
Return on Assets	- 4.8 %

Source: Selected Statistical Reports of Jurong Seaport; Authors, 2020

Analysis of Planned Scenarios

From the foregoing discussion on the market conditions of Jurong Port, the risk of market obsolescence poses a significant obstacle to the Port's growth. In response, Jurong Port has the choice to well undertake either of the following two planned scenarios:

Scenario 1, where the Jurong Port is planned to become a full-fledged container seaport like the Seaport of Hong Kong and the PSA Corporation, or

Scenario 2, where the Jurong Port is planned to become a "Maritime Industrial and Logistics Park" (MILP).

While Scenario 1 is envisaged in the steady state, Scenario 2 entails that Jurong Port becomes not only a marine terminal for cargo transit but also becomes an integrated unit that encompasses logistics and industrial functions (Ho *et. al.*, 1993). The economic development conception in support of Scenario 2 is the physical transformation of the Seaport of Rotterdam into the logistics centre for the entire River Rhine hinterland region. Taylor (1974) proposes a similar conception, known as the maritime industrial development areas (MIDAS), as the economic developmental strategy for seaport development in the United Kingdom. In Japan, seaports are envisaged to be the vital catalyst for both national and regional development, where seaports are strategically developed as integrated complexes with multiple functions for industry, commerce, communication, public services, housing and recreation (Seaports and Harbours in Japan, 1993). The US showcases its seaport sector to expand into markets like warehousing, commercial developments and airports. Closely following such directional and strategic showcasing include the Seaport of New York and the Seaport of New Jersey (Borrone, 1995).

As a result, several strategic infrastructure investment measures can be considered by Singapore's Jurong Port in order to realize the 5-prong MILP strategy of Scenario 2:

1. To reposition the existing business of handling the domestic import and export of steel products, heavy lifts and project cargoes as a regional "stockist". In addition, it is essential to develop the international transhipment of such traffic by fully leveraging its 16m deep water berths that can handle 150,000 DWT vessels.
2. To provide better facilities and more competitive business packages to enhance other conventional traffic like paper and pulp. Such provision provides the impetus to support the growth of container traffic.
3. To develop container freight stations and warehousing facilities to make Jurong Port a hub for all consolidation and distribution activities. This hub generates economic multipliers for other seaport services.
4. To minimise the market risk of the transhipment business via introducing and deepening 'domestic' cargo. It is essential

to attract value-added processing industrial activities and logistics activities to Jurong Port.
5. To carve for itself a major role for the import of other construction related raw materials and semi-finished products. Bricks, aggregates, sand, and pre-cast components should offer the base load and required stability to compensate for the relatively high volatility in the transhipment cargo market.

Risk Simulation & Model Estimations

On the basis of the above strategic infrastructure investment measures to enable the MILP strategy, a risk model is constructed under the conventional discounted cash flow (DCF) framework, with the annual income and expenditure simulated over a project life of 30 years. Injections into a strategic infrastructure investment measure are taken to be the initial purchase price of land, the price of other assets and the additional investments that are required to keep the physical assets and equipment serviceable, during the project life. The basic indicator of Jurong Port's performance is the cargo throughput (measured in tonnes). The cargo throughput is multiplied with the corresponding margins (in terms of S$ per tonne) in order to obtain the sales volume. Thereafter, the investment assessment criteria (parameters), namely, the internal rate of return (IRR) and the net present value (NPV) are to be determined.

Risk model simulations are conducted where the distribution of possible outcomes of the parameters in question (i.e. the IRR and NPV), is generated by re-estimating the model with randomly selected sets of values for the input variables. The risk simulations are activated using the Latin Hypercube sampling method, designed to accurately recreate the input probability distributions in fewer sampling iterations, relative to the less efficient Monte Carlo sampling method.

The key advantage of the Latin Hypercube sampling is the stratification of the input probability distributions that divides the cumulative curve into equal intervals on the cumulative probability scale. A sample is then randomly taken from each interval or stratification of the input distribution. The sampling is forced to represent values in each interval, and recreates the input probability distribution accordingly. Compared with the Monte Carlo method, a totally random process over the entire probability distribution, the resulting samples simulated under the Latin Hypercube method more accurately reflect the values of an input probability distribution. Two scenarios for cargo throughput are simulated under the resulting risk model and discussed below.

Scenario 1

Scenario 1 envisages the transformation of Singapore's Jurong Port into a full-fledged container terminal. The optimistic projection is that the throughput of the Asian seaports will double from about 52.2 mil TEUs in 1994 (Yong, 1995) to about 104 mil TEUs in 2000. Another optimistic projection is the annual growth of 20% p.a. to be achieved by PSA and Seaport of Hong Kong. This is historically achieved in the early 1990s. As the existing container throughput at Jurong Port is very low, a relatively stronger annual growth rate of 50% p.a. (up to a cap of 2.4 million TEU, the design capacity) is adopted. The growth rate for the conventional cargo market is taken to be 10% p.a. compounded until it reaches the maximum of 9 million tonnes p.a. In the case of bulk cargoes, a marginal growth rate of 3% (subject to a cap of 5.9 million tonnes) is presumed, owing to the need to set aside more seaport capacity for container handling. The initial input parameters to activate the risk simulation for Scenario 1 are provided in Table 2.6, and with the "Normal" operator denoting the normal probability distribution function.

Table 2.6. Input Parameters for Scenario 1

	Throughput at initial year (mil tonnes)	Average annual growth
Bulk	5.9	Normal (3%, 0.1* 3%)
Conventional	6.4	Normal (10%, 0.1* 10%)
Containers	3000 TEUs	Normal (50%, 0.5* 50%)

Source: Authors, 2005 & 2020

Scenario 2

Scenario 2 envisages the organic growth of Jurong Port's throughput performance. A 5% compounded growth rate (subject to a cap of 7.6 million tonnes owing to capacity provision) is presumed for bulk cargo, while taking into consideration the likelihood that Jurong Port sustains its vital role as the regional seaport hub for building materials like pre-cast components, bricks, specialty cement, etc. For conventional cargo, an annual growth rate of 20% is presumed and up to the maximum capacity of 17.9 million tonnes p.a., on the basis that Jurong Port eventually handles all the conventional cargo market in Singapore. The Port also enters new markets in steel products, vehicles, project cargoes and other neo-bulk markets. Containerised general cargo is presumed to be a complimentary market that grows at 10% p.a.. The initial input parameters to activate the risk simulation for Scenario 2 are provided in Table 2.7, with the "Normal" operator denoting the normal probability distribution function.

Table 2.7. Input Parameters For Scenario 2

	Throughput at initial year (mil tonnes)	Average annual growth
Bulk	5.9	Normal (5%, 0.1*5%)
Conventional	6.4	Normal (20%, 0.1*20%)
Containers	3000 TEUs	Normal (10%, 0.1*10%)

Source: Authors, 2005 & 2020

The base case assumes that land is purchased at the prevailing market price of S$792 per sqm per plot ratio. Sensitivity analysis is conducted on various land prices to determine how the IRR and NPV criteria would change as a result of changes in land price. Therefore, land price becomes an imperative output variable. The available land for allocation can either be leased on an initial lump sum payment or based on an annual rental payment, the prevailing practice in Jurong Seaport. The initial rent is taken to be S$44.6 per sqm p.a. with an annual increment of 3% expressed in the form of a normal distribution. Occupancy is assumed to be 20% initially and then to increase at 10% per annum until it reaches a long-term steady state level of 90%.

Scenario 2 is also dependent on the capacity projection of Jurong Port that in turn is dependent on several factors, namely, the total berth length, configuration of the berths, depth and configuration of the channel or waterways, deck loading capacity, type of handling equipment installed, the efficiency of the working system in terms of tonnes per hour and TEU per hour, the type and the mix of cargo being handled. On these factors, Jurong Port's present and future capacity are estimated according to the following 4-stepwise process:

1. Estimate the capacity of individual berths empirically, using data from FY95/96.
2. Determine the capacity of each type of berth as basic planning parameters.
3. Identify the potential for future berth development or reconfiguration.
4. Aggregate the capacities of the individual berths.

Table 2.6. Anticipation of Berth Capacity as a Planning Parameter

Berth no.	Throughput (freight tonnes)			Remarks
	Total throughput in FY 95/96	Monthly throughput of the max month * 12	Capacity for planning parameters	
1	110,759	308,184	300,000	River berth.
2	403,474	1,023,804	700,000	Coastal berth.

3	577,774	778,212		
4	678,552	920,256	800,000	Deep-water
5	604,297	796,656		multi-purpose
6	422,611	756,384		berth.
7	467,171	654,984		
8	427,418	719,556		
9	632,869	951,600	1,200,000	Bulk berth
10	796,381	1,455,600		
11	480,287	1,044,840		
12	933,553	1,194,552		
13	264,182	370,980	300,000	River berth.
14	868,436	1,116,000	1,000,000	Very deep multi-
15	1,011,780	1,307,220		purpose berth
16	852,105	1,135,236		
17	705,900	1,168,644		
18	953,687	1,377,672		
19	878,374	1,095,588		
20	192,950	253,380	300,000	River berth
21	124,655	160,896		

Source: Authors, 2005 & 2020

Based on the berth capacity planning parameter derived in Table 2.6, the future capacity of Jurong Port is estimated to be between 25.5 mil tonnes and 34.3 million tonnes[5], depending on the extent of container handling (shown in Table 2.7). Such an estimate incorporates a total of eight possible redevelopment and new development projects listed below but within Jurong Port's existing boundary[6]:

---

[5] The capacity of a container feeder berth is 250,000 TEU or 1.75 million tonnes of cargo p.a. Conversely, the capacity of a conventional berth is about 750,000 tonnes of cargo per year. In Hong Kong, the Sea-Land Orient Terminal (Slot) has achieved a throughput of 880,000 TEU in a single berth in 1995, and is expecting to hit 1.03 million TEU is 1996 (Business Times, 1996).

[6] Further expansion such as into Jurong Island is possible but this has not been included in this study.

1. Development of berth J26, lengthening of berth J14 and the decking up of the basin between them at an estimated cost of $60 million.
2. Development of berths J24, J25, and J12D to form a continuous quay of 1,117m or 6 berths at the north east face of the PDL (Pulau Dama Laut) island.
3. Extension of berths J12A such that berths J12 and J12A can be made into 2 conventional berths with a total length of 350m at an estimated cost of $60 million.
4. To develop a 20,000 sqm double storey warehouse to support berths J12 and J12A at an estimated cost of $24 million.
5. Development of new berths J12B and J12C at an estimated cost of $5 mil to rationalise all liquid bulk traffic at these berths.
6. Upgrading of berths J4 to J7 from the existing 20,000 dwt to 40,000 dwt capacity at an estimated cost of $50 million and development of river berths J1A, J1B, and J1C for coastal and riverine vessels at an estimated cost of $20 million.
7. Redevelopment of warehouses J9, J10, and J11 to renew 50,000 sqm of warehouse space at an estimated cost of $60 million, and development of a 250,000 sqm multi-storey warehouse complex at Jalan Buroh at an estimated cost of $600 million.
8. Installation of suitable handling equipment to improve productivity. Seaport equipment like gantry quay cranes or multi-purpose cranes cost about $7 mil a piece. <R: are these current plans or were they applicable/considered in 1996? If current, references are required>

Table 2.7. Present And Future Capacities Of Jurong Seaport (In Million Freight Tonnes)

Berth	Present situation		Future capacity without containers. Scenario '2'		Future capacity with containers. Scenario '1'		
	Bulk	Conv	Bulk	Conv	Bulk	Conv	Cont
1, 1A, 1B, 1C		0.3/berth		0.3/berth		0.3/berth	
2, 3		0.7/berth		0.7/berth		0.7/berth	
4-8		0.8/berth		0.8/berth		0.8/berth	
9-11	1.2/berth		1.2/berth		1.2/berth		
12	1.2			0.8		0.8	
12A				0.7		0.7	
12B				0.3		0.3	
12C				0.3		0.3	
12D				0.8		0.8	
13	0.3						
14-19		1.0/berth		1.0/berth			4 main berths: 1.6 TEU
20-21			Will be demolished in the redevelopment.				
22	2.0		2.0		2.0		
23	2.0		2.0				3 feeder berths: 0.8 TEU
24				0.8			
25				0.8			
26				0.8	2.0		
	9.1	11.7	7.6	17.9	5.6	9.5	19.2 (2.4 mil TEU)
Total	20.8		25.5		34.3		

Source: Authors, 2005 & 2020

Investment input variables to the Port investment project can be divided into two parts. First, the initial purchase price for the required piece of direct real estate, and the associated "goodwill" relating to the business. This initial purchase price is estimated to be S$1.58 billion (for a land area of 120 ha and other physical assets). Secondly, additional investments are required to upgrade and expand existing facilities to meet future demand. These investment projects are identified and their associated costs estimated on the basis of the following unit costs of Table 2.8. Where such investment projects are to be implemented, their project costs are inflated at a compounded rate of 3% to reflect the future value of money. As it is not possible to identify all the improvements and expansion investment projects for the next 30 years, some provision for such investments should still be catered for. Apart from the specific investment projects already identified, an amount equivalent to 15% of the operating surplus (i.e. gross revenue less the operating costs before tax) is set aside for further investments in capital assets. This 15% is chosen on the basis of empirical data in the last 5 years. The inference is that a similar level of development activities, in proportionate terms, is expected throughout the investment project life.

Table 2.8. Assumed Unit Cost of Additional Investments

Type of assets	Assumed unit cost of development
Berths	S$120,000 per m run.
Dolphins	S$50,000 per m run
Conventional warehouse	S$600 psm.
Multi-storey warehouses	S$1,200 psm
Unloading cranes	S$6 mil per unit.

Source: Authors, 2005 & 2020

The life of fixed physical capital assets is normally deemed to be 60 years. As the investment project life span is taken to be 30 years, there would be a residual value at the end of the 30-year period. While such residual value is not normally payable to the private investor at the end of the 30-year concession period in a "Built, Operate and Transfer" arrangement, a similar kind of consideration may well be extended in terms of a discount to the upfront premium for say land. However, the quantification of such a discount is not an exact science and there will always be problems associated with market forces, with possible capital gains and with the question of whether the government or the concessionaire should be enjoying such gains if any. For simplicity but without compromising reality, the base case assumes that there is not to be any residual value for fixed capital assets at the end of the 30-year period. While the initial purchase price cannot be objectively determined, a schedule of the initial purchase price versus the projected returns can be imputed to enhance decision-making or as a basis for valuation.

In the imputation of the risk model's income stream, the gross revenue is taken to be the proxy of Jurong Port's tariff structure, and the gross expenditure is taken to be the proxy of the operating costs. The proxies are then weighted with respect to the different cargo markets to ascertain the corresponding tariffs as outlined and explained below:

Based on the FY 95/96 data,

Gross revenue = $72.8 mil.
Operating expenditure (i.e. excl. depreciation) = $26.4 mil.
Total throughput = 12.27 mil tonnes.
Bulk cargo throughput = 5.86 mil tonnes or 48% of total.
Conventional cargo throughput = 6.39 mil tonnes or 52% of total.

Therefore,

Revenue due to bulk cargo = $34.9 mil
Assumed price of bulk cargo services = $34.9 mil / 5.86 mil tonnes
= $5.96/tonne.   (2.1)

Revenue due to conventional cargo = $37.9 mil
Assumed price of conventional cargo = $37.9 mil / 6.39 mil tonnes
= $5.93 / tonne.   (2.2)

Expenditure due to bulk cargo = $17.1 mil
Assumed cost of bulk cargo services = $12.7 mil / 5.86 mil tonnes
= $2.17/tonne.   (2.3)

Revenue due to conventional cargo = $13.7 mil
Assumed cost of conventional cargo services = $13.7 mil / 6.39 mil tonnes
= $2.14 / tonne.   (2.4)

Comparing steps (2.1) and (2.3),

$\text{Cost}_{\text{bulk cargo}} / \text{Price}_{\text{bulk cargo}}$ = 2.17 / 5.96
= 36 %

Surplus of bulk cargo services = $5.96 - $2.17
= $ 3.79 / tonne. (2.5)

Comparing steps (2;2) and (2.4),

$\text{Cost}_{\text{conventional cargo}} / \text{Price}_{\text{conventional cargo}}$ = 2.14 / 5.93
= 36 %

Surplus of conventional cargo services = $5.93 - $2.14
= $3.79 / tonne. (2.6)

As Jurong Port does not handle containers in significant amount, PSA's figures are used to impute the price and operating cost for this market. The following analysis can thus be derived:

Operating revenue = $1.93 billion
Operating cost = $1.1 billion
Throughput = 11.85 million TEU.

Therefore,
Assumed price per TEU = $1.93 billion / 11.85 million
= $163 /TEU
assume 8 tonnes/TEU, = $20.4 / tonne (2.7)

Assumed cost per TEU = $1.1 billion / 11.85 million
= $93 / TEU
assume 8 tonnes/TEU, = $11.6 / tonne (2.8)

Comparing steps (2.5) and (2.6),

$\text{Cost}_{\text{container}} / \text{Price}_{\text{container}}$ = 11.6 / 20.4
= 57%

Surplus of container services = $163/TEU - $93/TEU
= $70/TEU
= $8.8 / tonne. (2.9)

Comparing steps (2.5) and (2.6) with (2.9), it can be seen that the absolute margin for container services more than doubles that of conventional and bulk cargo services. Such observation is good evidence to recommend that Jurong Port pursue appropriate strategies in order to configure itself to serve the container market as well. The corresponding land rental and net income from other seaport operations (i.e. after deducting the operating expenses) are then summed to derive the total net surplus.

Risk Simulation Results

The impact of the risk model simulations on the IRR and NPV investment criteria is examined with respect to the various planned scenarios formulated earlier. The Kurtosis and skewness of the two investment criteria are inspected for their variability, which in turn indicate the riskiness of the scenario projections. Kurtosis is a measure of the shape of the distribution by indicating how flat or narrowly peaked will the distribution be. The higher the kurtosis value, the more peaked the distribution. However, skewness indicates the degree of asymmetry of a distribution. The projected returns of Scenario 1 are presented in Table 2.9.

Table 2.9. Scenario 1: Jurong Seaport Being a Container Seaport

	Min	Mean	Max	Std dev.	Kurtosis	Skewness
IRR	0.9%	5.3%	12.6%	1.5%	3.6	0
NPV	-$739m	$1550m	$33309m	$1454m	98	6.1

Source: Authors, 2005 & 2020

Table 2/9 should be compared with the simulation results as single point estimates, i.e. whenever the input parameters are expressed as probability distributions, they are each expressed as a point estimate in terms of the mean of the probability distributions. The projected returns comprise the

IRR = 6% and NPV = $1521 mil.

The projected returns of Scenario 2 are presented in Table 2.10.

Table 2.10. Scenario 2 - Jurong Seaport Being A MILP

	Min	Mean	Max	Std dev.	Kurtosis	Skewness
IRR	2.4%	4.5%	12.1%	1.1%	6.0	1
NPV	-690m	$706m	$7486m	$08m	26	3.4

Source: Authors, 2005 & 2020

Similarly, the simulation results with the single point estimates consisting of

IRR = 4%;   NPV = $580 mil.

Based on a discount rate of 7%[7], the simulation results suggest that the investment project is not viable when it is evaluated under both scenarios. Nevertheless, when compared to each other, Scenario 1 that envisages Jurong Seaport as a pure container terminal in the footsteps of the Seaport of Hong Kong and the PSA, is projected to generate slightly higher returns.

Constraint optimisation

In addition to scenario planning, the question of "how much of each cargo market should Jurong Port allocate its limited resources?" can be addressed by non-linear constraint programming. Therefore, the specific research problem to be resolved is non-linear in nature. Under constraint optimisation, the objective function is to maximise IRR subject to the following eqs (2.1) to (2.3):

$$\text{Throughput}_{BULK} + \text{Throughput}_{CONVENTIONAL} + \text{Throughput}_{CONTAINERS}$$
$$=< 34.3 \text{ mil tonnes, which is the maximum capacity of JP.} \quad (2.1)$$

---

[7] JTC adopts a discount rate of 7% in evaluation of capital projects. This is also used as the 'hurdle' rate as it is also taken as the cost of money.

Throughput$_{BULK}$ >= 5 mil tonnes.
This is to cater to the basic imports for the domestic markets like cement and essential raw materials for the industries. (2.2)

Throughput$_{CONVENTIONAL}$ >= 15 mil tonnes.
This is to cater to the basic volume generated by the domestic market. (2.3)

The variables are of course the throughput of the various markets in each year's throughput of the investment project life.

Resolving the above equations, under the non-linear constraint programming algorithm produces the following solutions:

Bulk cargo = 5 mil tonnes ;
Conventional cargo = 15 mil tonnes ;
Containers = 14.3 mil tonnes.

The solutions are expected because other than having to satisfy the minimum requirements to serve the local bulk and conventional cargo markets, all other resources of Jurong Port should be allocated to serve the more lucrative container market. The constraint programming algorithm is an appropriate alternative approach to estimate the value of Jurong Port's assets, which do not have direct market comparables. PSA is not a good comparable for valuation purposes because it is primarily a container seaport whereas Jurong Port is a multi-purpose seaport. Moreover, there is no alternative use of the land in the Jurong Port, as the government has safeguarded the land for seaport use.

From a potential investor's point of view, and given the freedom to purchase Jurong Port or other of its assets (for e.g. its industrial land or commercial buildings), there is no reason why the expected return on Jurong Port should differ substantially from the expected returns of other possible candidates for investments. However, and owing to the specificity of land in Jurong Seaport for seaport use, an investor, who is to purchase Jurong Port, has to evaluate the risks of holding such an asset that can only generate returns from its seaport use. Table 2.11 presents the results obtained from the non-linear constraint programming algorithm by varying the prices of the existing assets and additional land, while maintaining the other variables in the same manner as discussed earlier.

Table 2.11. Schedule of Desired Return Versus Initial Purchase Price

	Desired returns				
	7%	10%	15%	20%	25%
Price of existing assets.	918	437	8	-210	-335
Price of additional of land	871	871	871	871	871
Total	1,789	1,308	879	661	536

NB. All figures in S$ million. Source: Authors, 2005 & 2020

Table 2.11 shows that in order to generate returns of 20%, not only will an investor be unable to pay for the existing assets, but that he will need to be compensated for any future business risk that he may be exposed to. In theory, the amount of subsidy provided by the government, whether in absolute or relative terms, may be envisaged to be the payment for external benefits (i.e. positive economic externality) that such a large infrastructure investment will spill over to society at large. However, if the cost of capital is taken to be 7%, which may be construed as the hurdle rate or the break-even rate, then Jurong Port's existing assets will only be worth S$918 million. This is far lower than the estimated S$1.576 billion obtained from the replacement cost approach.

Limitations

While simulation has the advantage of taking into account all the uncertainty inherent in a planned scenario, it has two drawbacks. First, in modelling real-world situations, the form of the probability distribution of a random input variable may be deduced theoretically on the basis of physical considerations, or may be inferred empirically on the basis of observed data. Extensive data on similar past projects must therefore be available to support such inferences.

Where there is incomplete documentation, the assumed market (business) growth rates, which are the main uncertain parameters in the model simulations, are based on intuitive judgement after consulting the best practices and the practitioners in the seaport industry (as depicted in Fig 2.9). Future examinations may help to improve this difficulty via econometric modelling for e.g. to link the business projections with better defined macro-economic indicators like GDP growth, and trade figures between countries.

Constraint optimisation (linear or non-linear programming algorithms) may offer some insight to derive an optimum initial purchase price for the assets of Jurong Port, as well as to determine the optimal allocation of resources to the different markets. Thus, constraint optimisation serves to facilitate more informed decision-making by the investor.

Fig 2.9. The Flows of Experience

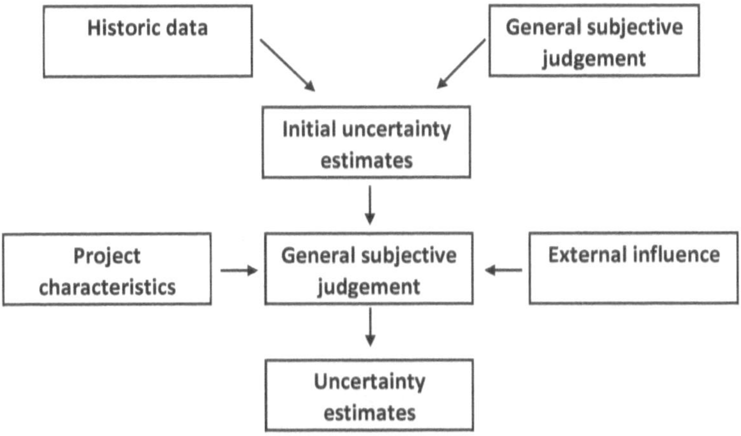

Source: Simister, 1994; Authors, 2020

Sensitivity analysis and scenario planning are by far the most meaningful methodologies or approaches for dealing with uncertainty. It is not to imply that simulation should be regarded as a last resort when all other approaches have failed. However, only when a user-investor is fully experienced in other simpler approaches, will the user-investor be able to benefit from the use of more complex approaches.

Concluding Remarks

The process of risk management has been demonstrated with Jurong Port as the case study. A uniquely formulated theoretical framework of analysis provides the basis for the identification of risks in determining Jurong Port's strategic options for growth.

Two major categories of risks confronting Jurong Port are identified. The first is the uncertainty in the prediction of future rates of increase in seaport tariffs, the volumes of the various markets (businesses), and the implication of the rising trend in cargo containerisation. All these are exogenous factors that are mostly uncontrollable. The second is the risk relating to the internal weaknesses of Jurong Port like costing, pricing and the operating systems, that if not adequately addressed, will affect Jurong Seaport's competitiveness.

As a result of the foregoing considerations, there are basically two investment strategies for Jurong Port to choose from, namely, to become a full-fledged container terminal (i.e. Scenario 1) or to configure itself as a maritime industrial and logistics park (MILP) (i.e. Scenario 2). These strategies are subject to quantitative simulations, which are conducted by scrutinising the variability of the projected returns of the investment for each scenario, through the Monte Carlo risk simulation model. Furthermore, constraint optimisation under the non-linear algorithm is employed to determine the resources to be allocated among the potential cargo markets. The results affirm the Monte Carlo model simulations with respect to returns on investment.

The results indicate that although the projected returns of the "MILP" is not as impressive as the "container terminal" strategy, nevertheless, the variability of the former strategy's returns and hence the risks, are very much lower than those of the latter strategy. Therefore, the MILP strategy is recommended for Jurong Port and this will enable the Port to secure a firm foundation with respect to the localised industries, and to entrench its hub operations.

In drawing on the above recommendations, a sense of reality in view of Jurong Port's small size and limited capacity is to be taken into consideration. Significant innovations accompanied by major investments have been proposed to revitalise an otherwise aging national estate. By way of repackaging and rebranding it as the MILP rather than as a pure container terminal for obvious reasons of competence and strategic 'wholesomeness' of the former, should ultimately generate new demands and lift Jurong Port onto a new and high path of growth. Accordingly, the hosting of value-adding, processing and industrial activities, of the regional distribution centre and warehousing, have been identified as necessary compliments to reduce the elasticity of the otherwise extremely elastic and competitive transhipment business[8]. Furthermore, it is sensible to question the rationale for Singapore to focus only on container traffic particularly in the light of the countries in the region being inclined to handle their own domestic cargoes. Jurong Port's sustained viability may well be to redirect its resources and efforts to transform itself into the MILP while keeping a constant look out for niche opportunities to secure container traffic for e.g. through the structuring of "back-to-back agreements", covering terms like throughput guarantees and the exclusive use of Jurong Port with global shipping lines.

While the foregoing set of arguments and recommendations are developed on the basis of Jurong Port as the case study, they may well be extended to and/or modified for the development and investment of seaports, particularly in the developing countries that are in urgent need of large-scale infrastructure upgrading.

---

[8] Hutchison Seaport Holdings (HPH) which is the world's largest privately owned container terminal operator, adopts a policy of not investing in facilities that rely on transhipment (Brevetti, 1996).

References

AFP. "Samy Vellu urges government to agree to 33% hike in toll". In <u>The Business Times</u>. 20th November, 1995. Singapore.

AHMED, Raisuddin., DONOVAN, Cynthia. "Issues of Infrastructural Development: A Synthesis of the Literature". International Food Policy Research Institute. Washington D.C. 1992.

ALMAZAN, Alec. "Subic authority in no-win position". Business Times. 23 Aug 1996.

ALMAZAN, Alec. "Philippones in 492b-peso seaport upgrading plan". Busines Times. 29 August 1996.

ANDERSON, S D. "Project quality and project managers". <u>In International Journal of Project Management</u>. Vol 10. No 3. August 1992.

ANG, Alfredo H.S., TANG, Wison H. "Probability Concepts In Engineering Planning And Design. Volume 1 - Basic Principles." John Wiley & Sons. 1995.

ARLT, Wolfhard H., "The treatment of uncertainty in seaport planning". HPTI - Hamburg Seaport Training Institute, GmbH, Hamburg, 1986.

BECKER, H. A., VAN DOORN, J. W. "Scenarios in an organisational Perspective". In <u>Futures</u>. December, 1987.

BOOKER, Jane M., BRYON, Maurice C. "Decision Analysis In Project Management: An Overview." In <u>IEEE Transactions on Engineering Management</u>. Vol EM-32. No 4. Nov 1990.

BORRONE, Lillian C. "Seaports are key to stable economies". In <u>VIA Seaport of New York - New Jersey</u>. Jul/Aug 1995. P6.

BREVETTI, Francine. "Hutchison hungry for privatisation deals". Seatrade Review. September 1996.

BRIGHAM, Eugene F., GAPENSKI, Louis C. "Financial Management - Theory and Practice". 6th Edition. The Dryden Press. 1977.

BROCKINGTON, R. B. "Financial Management". DP Publications Ltd. 4th Edition, 1987.

CANO, A del. "Continous project feasibility study and continuous project risk assessment". In International Journal of Project Management. Vol 10. No 3. Aug 1992.

CARTER, D. E. "Evaluating commercial projects". In Research Management. Vol XXV, pp 26-30, 1982.

CHAPMAN, Chris., COOPER, Dale. "Risk Analysis for Large Projects, Models, Methods, and Cases." John Wiley & Sons. 1987.

CHECKLAND, Peter., SCHOLES, Jim. "Soft Systems Methodology in Action".John Wiley & Sons. 1990.

CLARK, R C., PLEDGER, M., NEEDLER, H M J. "Risk analysis in the evaluation of non-aerospace projects". Project Management. Vol. 8 No. 1. February 1990.

ELIAS, Rahita. "PSA in talks to manage new container seaport in Myanmar seaport". Business Times. 22 Sep 1995.

ELIAS, Rahita. "Singapore firm building Myanmar seaport". Business Times. 22 Sep 1995.

FUNTOWICZ, Silvio O., RAVETZ, Jerome R. "Uncertainty and Quality in Science for Policy." Kluwer Academic Publishers. 1990.

GALAI, Ahmed, JONES, Leroy., TANDON, Pankai., VOGELSANG, Ingo. "Welfare consequences of selling public enterprises - An empirical analysis. Oxford University Press. 1994. (NUS: HD 3850 Wel).

GRAY, Tony. "European Maritme centres: wooing far east shipping lines". Busness Times. 29 August 1996.

HARGITAY, Stephen E., YU, Shi-Ming. "Property Investment Decisions - A Quantitative Approach". E & FN SPON. 1993.

HARRISION, Ian W. "Capital Investment Appraisal". McGraw-Hill. 1973.

HERTZ, David B., THOMAS, Howard. "Risk Analysis and its applications". Johy Wiley and Sons. 1984.

HIGGINS, B. "Economic development". New York. Norton. 1959.

HIRSCHMAN, A. O. "Strategy of economic development". New Haven, Conn., U.S.A. Yale University Press.

HO, Kim Hin, David. "An Econometric Model Simulating the Effects of Seaport Policy and National Economic Development in Singapore". Journal of Real Estate and Construction, 1994. 4: 29 - 47.

HO, M. W. "Castrol Singapore Pte. Ltd." Unpublished internal document of Jurong Town Corporation submitted to the Policy, Planning and Development Committee. 4 Nov 1995.

HO, M.W. "Jurong Seaport Business Plan, 1993- 2004". Unpublished internal document of Jurong Town Corporation. Oct 1993.

HO, M. W. "Refurbishment and Upgrading of Berth J8 to J12 at Jurong Seaport". Unpublished internal document of Jurong Town Corporation. Oct 1994.

HO, M.W. "Impact of new dockage charges". Unpublished internal document of Jurong Town Corporation. 21 Aug 199.

HO, M.W. "Roadlink to Southern Island". Unpublished internal document of Jurong Town Corporation. Oct 1996.

HO, M. W., KALLIMASSIAS, G., KALOGIANNIS, G. "Proposed BEST PRACTICE Project Risk Management". Unpublished master's dissertation. School of Management, University of Lancaster, U.K. 1992.

HUGHES, David. "Can general cargo ships survive the age of containerisation?". Business Times. 26 Jun 1996.

HUGHES, David. "Singapore and HK both face competition for hub seaport status". Business Times. 22 Jul 1996.

HUSEBY, A B., SKOGEN, S. "Dynamic risk analysis: the DynRisk concept". In International Journal of Project Management. Vol. 10. No. 3. August 1992.

HULL, J K. "Application of risk analysis techniques in proposal assessment". Project Management. Vol. 8. No. 3. August, 1990.

JTC. Jurong Town Corporation internal documents and correspondances with the Auditor General's Office. Filed under "Audit Matters" in the Jurong Seaport Registry. 1994.

JONES, Clive Vaugham. "Financial risk analysis of infrastructure deb: the case of water and power investments". Quorum Books. 1991.

KAGAN, Robert. "Patterns of Seaport Development". Research Reseaport UCB-ITS-RR-90-13. University of California at Berkeley. Institute of Transpotation Studies. October, 1990.

KAWASAKI, YOSHIKAZU. "Overall concept of seaport planning". International Seaport Cargo distribution Associaiton of Japan.

KLAMMER, T., "The Association of Capital Budgeting techniques with firm performance". In <u>Accounting Review</u>. April, 1973, pp 353-364.

KOBYLARZ, Korina (Captain). "Establishing of Departmen of Defense Program Management Body of Knowledge". In <u>Project Management Journal</u>. Vol XXIII. No. 1. March 1992.

KUDO, Kazuo. "Implementation of Seaport development policy in Japan: Problems and countermeasures". In "<u>Seaport Development Policy - Proceedings of a seminar-cum-study tour, Japan, October 1984</u>". ESCAP Seaport Development Series No. 7. United Nations. 1985.

LEWIS, W.A. "Strategy of economic growth". London. Allen and Unwin. 1955.

MacDONALD, John. "Load centres - How carriers driven concentration will affect concentration and seaports." <u>Lloyd's List Maritime Asia</u>. June 1996.

MARKOWITZ, Harry M. "Seaportfolio Selection - Effiicient diversification of investments". John Wiley & Sons. 1959.

MIKKELSEN, Hans. "Risk Management in product development projects". <u>In Project Management</u>. Vol 8. No. 4. Nov 1990.

MUSTAFA, Muhammad A., AL-BAHAR, Jamal, F. "Project Risk Assessment Using the Analytic Hierarchy Process". <u>In IEEE Transactions on Engineering management</u>. Vol. 38. No. 1. February 1991.

NICOLO, E. "Metaproject analysis: multiagent virtual project networks for strategic decisions in preplannin". International Journal of Project Management. Vol 11. No.4 November, 1993.

NURSKE, R. "Problems of capital formation in underdeveloped countries." New York. Oxford University Press. 1953.

PETERS, Edgar E. "Chaos and order in the capital markets - A New View of Cycles, Prices, and Market Volatility". John Wiley & Sons. 1991.

PETERS, Hans, J. "Private Sector Involvement in East and Southeast Asian Seaports - An Overview of Contractural Arrangements". Paper presented at AsiaSeaport'96 held at Kowloon Shangri-la Hotel in Hong Kong from 16 Sep 1996 to 19 Sep 1996.

PINTO, Jeffrey K., MANTEL, Samuel J. JR. "The Causes of Project Failure". In IEEE Transactions on Engineering Management. Vol 37. No. . November 1990.

PLYMTON, Anne., BRUNKER, Don. "Impediments to private provision of infrastructure". In Occasional Paper 7, Private Provision of Economic Infrastructure, Conference papers and proceedings from the BIE infrastructure forum, Canberra 1-2 June 1992. pp 185 - 216. 1992. (NUS, HC 79 Cap.Pr)

SEAPORTER, Michael. "The case for private provision of infrastructure in Australia?". In "Occasional Paper 7, Private Provision of Economic Infrastructure, Conference papers and proceedings from the BIE infrastructure forum, Canberra 1-2 June 1992". Bureau of Industry Economics. p39-55. 1992.

RAJ, Conrad. "Guoco to take majority stake in Subic venture". Business Times. 23 Aug 1996.

REN, H. "Risk lifecycle and risk relationships on construction projects". In <u>International Journal of Project Management</u>. Vol. 12. No. 2. 1994.

ROBERTS, Karlene H., ROUSSEAU, Denise M. "Research in Nearly Failure-free, High-Reliability Organizations: Having the bubble." <u>IEEE Transactions on Engineering Management</u>. Vol 36. No. 2. May 1989.

ROSENSTEIN-RODAN, P. N. "Problems of industrialization of eastern and southeastern Europe". <u>The Economic Journal</u>. 53. June1943.

SADGROVE, Kit. "The complete guide to business risk management". Gower Publishing Limited. 1996.

SAMUELSON, P. "The pure theory of public expenditure". <u>Review of Economis and Statistics</u>. 36(4): 387-89.

SCHUYLER, John R. "Decision Analysis in Projects: Modeling Techniques - Part II". PMNETwork, October 1994.

SCOTTO, Marie. "Project budgests are not functional budgets". In <u>PMNET</u>. March 1994.

SEAFARER. "Changes on the horizon with MPA as new maritime guardian". Business Times. 17 Jul 1996.

SEAFARER. "Seaports should operate like all other money making businesses". Business Times. 4th October 1995.

SEAFEARER. "Singapore must act now to maintain its dominant hub seaport position". Business Times. 25 Sep 1996.

SEILER, R K. "Reasoning about uncertainty in certain expert systems: implications for project management applications". In Project Management. Vol 8, No 1. February 1990.

SEN, Basudeb. "Infrastructure financing - Desing for effective partnership". Conference paper presented on behalf of Unit Trust of India during the INVESTSEAPORT Conference organised by the Confederation of Indian Industries in Madras from 8th - 10th Apr 1996.

SIMISTER, Steve J. "Usage and benefits of project risk analysis and management". In International Journal of Project Management.

SLAVIN, Terry. "All systems go for virtual seaport". Business Times. 15 Jul 1996.

TAN K. B., HO, M. W. "Steel stockyard and transhipment centre in Jurong Seaport". Unpublished internal document of Jurong Town Corporation. Apr 1996.

TAN, K. S. "Asia takes the risk of allowing infrastructure role for private sector." The Straits Time. 28 Oct 1994.

TAN, Tarn How. "Singapore will focus on distribution services in north-east China". The Straits Times. 15th Jul 1996.

TAN, Willie. "Research Methods in Real Estate and Construction". School of Building & Estate Management, National Univesity of Singapore. 1995. p3: Types of research.

TAYLOR, L.G. "Seaports - An introduction to their place and purpose". Brown, Son & Ferguson, Ltd., Nautical Publishers. 1974. (JTC lib: 387.1 Tay).

TEH, Hooi Ling. "Singapore investors too optimistic about China business: survey". Business Times. 28 Aug 1996.

JONES, Clive Vaugham. "Financial risk analysis of infrastructure debt: the case of water and power investments". p10. Quorum Books. 1991.

WALTERS, Alan A. "The Value of Land". In DUNKERLEY, Harold B. (Editor). "Urban Land Policy - Issues and Opseaportunities". Oxford University Press. 1983.

WEST, Staniland. "Feasibility Analyses, An Explanation!". In <u>Cost Engineering</u>. Vol. 35/No. 3. March 1993.

WINSTON, Clifford., BOSWORTH, Barry. "Public Infrastructure Investment". In <u>Occasional Paper 7, Private Provision of Economic Infrastructure, Conference papers and proceedings from the BIE infrastructure forum, Canberra 1-2 June 1992</u>. Bureau of Industry Economics. p103-133. 1992.

YONG, Mei Fong. "Asian Seaports may face demand of 104m boxes in 2000". Business Times, 4 October 1996.

YONG, Mei Fong. "Bid to combine Shanghai, Ningbo into hub seaport". Business Times. 15th July, 1996.

YOUNGSON, A.J. "Overhead capital: a study in development economics." Edinburgh University Press. 1967.

Other Relevant Publications

_____. "@RISK - Risk Analysis and Simulation Add-In for Microsoft Excel or Lotus 1-2-3. Palisade Corporation. 1 Feb 1995.

_____. "Investment needed for expansion". Business Times. 15th July, 1996.

_____. "Malaysia to allot M$4.7 b for seaport facilities". Business Times. 26 Jun 1996.

_____. "New Seaport for Johor Straits". Straits Shipper. August 28 - Septermber 3, 1995.

_____. "New toll rates will boost highway firm's cash flow". The Straits Times. 11 August, 1996.

_____. "Philippines opens its first dedicated grains terminal." Business Times. 25 Jun 1996.

_____. "Seaports and Harbours in Japan - 1993". Ministry of Transseaport, The Government of Japan. 1993.

_____. "Seaport Klang hits 23% growth mark." Straits Shipper. 29 Jul - 4 Aug, 1996.

_____. "Seaport Klang now free commercial zones." The Straits Times. 21 Jun 1996.

_____. "Seaport Klang offers lesson on privatisation for PSA". The Straits Times. 21 Jun 1996.

_____. "Private Sector-led growth". Straits Shipper. May 13 - 19, 1996.

_____. "Private sector to fund most infrastructure projects". Business Times, 3 Sep 1996.

_____. "PSA chalks up impressive 22% rise in operating surplus to record $820m". The Straits Times. 21 Jun 1996.

_____. "Sea-Land Orient Terminals set to score world first". Business Times. 25 Jun 1996.

CHAPTER 3

STRUCTURAL DYNAMICS IN THE POLICY PLANNING OF LARGE INFRASTRUCTURAL INVESTMENT UNDER THE COMPETITIVE ENVIRONMENT – THE CONTEXT OF SEAPORT THROUGHPUT AND CAPACITY

Chapter 3 takes cognisance that seaport performance in a steady state is inherently dynamic because seaport performance involves multiple feedback processes, which produce self-correcting or self-reinforcing side effects of decisions (Sterman 1992). The feedback processes can become more complex and dynamic under the influence of an economy's external sector and the domestic economy. Understanding these feedback processes within a system of cause-and-effect relationships helps to provide an analytic solution to the causal loop framework of analysis. Within the causal loop framework, many factors are envisaged to affect seaport throughput via a system of cause-and effect relations. In the case of Hong Kong where land, waterfront and sea space resources are scarce, the competition for their utilisation would be between using them for eaport developments and alternative economic generating uses like housing, commercial, or industrial activities. Such competitive utilisation of scarce physical resources becomes an even more complex issue if one takes into consideration the progressive transformation of Hong Kong into an essentially tertiary economy in which its manufacturing sector produces physical goods that contributes to only 15% of its GDP (PMB, 2001). As a result, there is little or declining domestically induced demand for seaport services to handle physical goods originating from or destined to Hong Kong *per se*.

Although Hong Kong is still the world's busiest seaport, transhipment cargo comprises roughly 60% of its seaport throughput. The bulk of this cargo class is destined to and originates from Mainland China (Ho, 1995). It is therefore not surprising that there are proponents of the development strategy that Hong Kong should relinquish its hub seaport status to the emerging seaports along the Pearl River delta in mainland China; and to subsequently focus its land and capital resources on other developments that could be better aligned to its comparative advantage instead (Headlands, *et. al.* 2004).

Therefore, a major challenge in policy planning regarding the Seaport of Hong Kong is to address the question of whether or not there is a sustained future role for the Seaport from the urban planning and development perspectivea. In other words, given that there are four major seaports in the Pearl River Delta region, and that their throughputs have been expanding at a rate of about 50% between the first half of 2001 and the first half of 2002 (Business Times, 2002), would there then be any need to continue to expand the Seaport of Hong Kong? The answer would largely depend on the anticipated throughput for the Seaport and the opportunity cost of alternative usage of the land earmarked for seaport use. These two considerations would be unique criteria relevant to the issue of sustainable development of Hong Kong (Jeon *et. al.*, 2006; Loo & Chow, 2006).

The conventional method of anticipating seaport throughput is via the multiple regression analysis (MRA) approach that investigates key external factors influencing throughput, and is solved by the method of least squares. The other methods include input-output analysis, a procedure that investigates the linkages between domestic factors and the throughput growth; while the structural econometric model examines the interaction of key external and domestic factors on the throughput growth. All three methods are based on economic theory and principles although they are estimated on historical trends. Therefore, the three methods would be unable to reflect the impact and the growth opportunities presented by new factors that may come into play, during the period when the anticipated seaport throughputs are required. For e.g., it would not be able to deal with the question of how seaport expansion or the emergence of new markets and competitors would affect the throughput of a seaport of interest. However, it is recognised that there have been attempts like the error correction model approach to improve such forecasting attempts (Hui *et. al.*, 2004).

In policy modelling, it is imperative to disentangle a highly focused set of the likely internal and external factors attributable to the active policy of sustained investment in upgrading seaport infrastructure. The other factors, that are outside the focussed set and that are attributable to other active public policies like industrial, urban public expenditure policies (on roads, rail, etc), would have to be excluded. Hence, the significance of Seaport policy strength is highlighted in the policy modelling to take advantage of the growth opportunities in sea transport services.

As a result, Chapter 3 introduces a dynamic seaport performance model (DPPM), which adopts a rigorous and robust system dynamic modelling approach, through the formulation of a causal loop framework applied in the context of economic, social and environmental systems (Richardson 1985). This causal loop framework is concerned with the feedback process and the dynamic behaviour of the throughput for the Seaport of Hong Kong. In this way, it can deal with the dynamic complexities, in deepening the understanding of the performance of the seaport system, i.e. the Seaport of Hong Kong.

On the basis of the DPPM simulation and analysis, an assessment can be undertaken to analyse whether or not seaport policy in the case of the capacity upgrading of the Seaport of Hong Kong should be extended to beyond the present nine terminals? Alternatively, can Hong Kong be better off by devolving the incremental capacity requirements to its neighbouring Seaports in the Pearl River Delta region and to then focus its resources on other developments? Even if such a decision ise made, would the existing level of throughput in Hong Kong be sustained for an indefinite period? Would there be the unintended side effects like the "decay" of seaport throughput, which may well set in overtime owing to the loss of growth opportunities? Further to the DPPM, planning methodologies like genetic algorithm can be adopted to search for optimal future land-use and transportation plans for the City (Balling *et.al.* 1999).

Chapter 3 discusses the entire process of examination including system conceptualization, model formation, equation simulation, model validation and policy analysis. This Chapter also examines the rigorous model specification of the DPPM by addressing the key components of stocks, flows, and feedback structure. Various new and robust concepts are also discussed, namely, the causal loop framework, the causal loop diagram, and how these are used as the building blocks to construct the DPPM. The next (third) section discusses the model estimation of the DPPM and its meaningful potential for scenario planning, i.e. the scenario analysis process, inclusive of the appropriate policy levers. The fourth section concludes Chapter 3's findings.

The Dynamic Seaport Performance Model (DPPM) Model

The DPPM's system dynamics are discussed in the light of the above step-wise and analytical process. The conceptual foundation originates from the ideas in the Ford and Sterman model (1997). A loop in the causal loop framework in effect depicts the feedback structure of a direct real (DRE) market for instance. The loop is a map that depicts the causal links amongst the DRE variables, with arrows from a cause to an effect. The effect can be a positive sign or a negative sign at the end of the arrow. For the positive sign, the loop is a reinforcing loop, (i.e. a positive feedback loop), that can turn into a runaway situation – i.e. a loop that is out of control in the extreme situation. For the negative sign, the loop is a negative feedback loop that stabilizes the loop into a steady state to some extent.

On feedback strategy to the loop, the positive signs in the loop dominate in some occasions while the negative signs dominate in others. The principle of loop dominance is observed. A mix in between can occur. Therefore, the loop (i.e. a diagram of the causal loop framework) depicts the structure of a DRE market's dynamics at work. Stocks and flows represent the underlying structure of a market or an economic sector. Stocks and Flows track the accumulation of material, price, capital value (CV), rent and information as they move through a market (itself a system). Stocks represent the inventory of say, a real estate product, debt, employment, etc. Stocks characterise the state of the market and generate the information (with or without time delays), upon which decisions are based. The decisions then alter the rates of flows, altering the stocks and closing the feedback loop in a market (system). Flows represent the rates of increase.

System Conceptualization

The Seaport of Hong Kong is a global maritime transhipment hub in East and North East Asia. The key unit of measurement of seaport throughput, including that

for the Seaport of Hong Kong is in terms of millions of TEU (twenty feet equivalent units) per year whereby TEU is the standard measurement of one twenty feet container. The key causal factors that would affect the throughput of the Seaport of Hong Kong can be broadly divided into two groups. The first group denotes the exogenous factors. These are the throughput that originates from mainland China and that throughput from Taiwan. The second group denotes the endogenous factors, i.e. Hong Kong's own domestically generated throughput. In the two factor groups of sea throughput, the demand is affected by the dynamic response to congestion as the price premium. In Fig 3.1, seaport congestion is plotted against the changing level of terminal handling charges in a graphical non-linear relationship, as an alternative to a least-square multiple regression analysis relationship. Intuitively and from prior experience and expert knowledge, the terminal handling charges are deemed to rise in tandem with rising congestion until such charges become excessive, and as part of the rationing process eases off subsequently to reach an equilibrium.

Each of the above two factor groups of seaport throughput and the sum of their transhipment volumes that take place at the Seaport of Hong Kong, represent the stocks of the system. Correspondingly, the levels of these throughputs change over time owing to changes in trade conditions. The changing throughput levels would be the flows of the system. Collectively, they interact dynamically to exert a demand on Hong Kong's Seaport infrastructure.

Fig 3.1. Graphical Relationship Between Congestion & Terminal Handling Charges

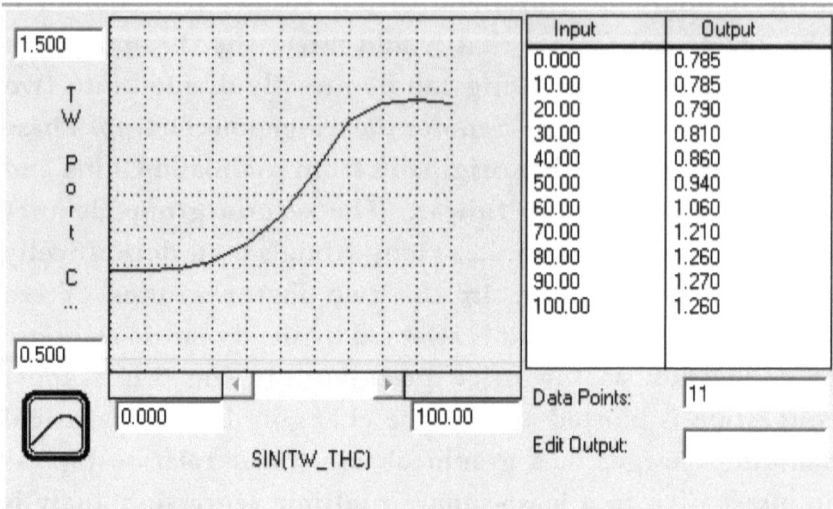

Source: ithink program, 2007; Authors, 2020

In other words,

$$\text{Total Hong Kong throughput, T'put}_{\text{Hong Kong}} (t)$$

$$= \int \text{T'put}_{\text{Hong Kong Domestic}} + \text{T'put}_{\text{Mainland Transhipment @ HK}} + \text{T'put}_{\text{Taiwan Transhipment @ HK}} \, dt \quad (3.1)$$

$$\text{T'put}_{\text{Hong Kong Domestic}}$$
$$= \int \text{HK\_Tput} (1 + \text{Growth}_{\text{Hong Kong Domestic}})^t (l_{HK}) (a_{HK}) \, dt \quad (3.2)$$

where,
(l_{HK}) represents various macro factors due to political and economic risks at HK, (a_{HK}) represents the impact of price premiums due to congestions at HK.

$$\text{T'put}_{\text{Mainland Transhipment @ HK}}$$
$$= \int \text{ML\_Tput} (1 + \text{Growth}_{\text{Mainland Transhipment @ HK}})^t (l_{ML}) (a_{ML}) \, dt \quad (3.3)$$

where,

(l_{ML}) **represents various macro factors due to political and economic risks at ML,** (a_{ML}) represents the impact of price premiums due to congestions at ML.

$$\text{T'put}_{\text{Taiwan Transhipment @ HK}} \quad (4)$$

$$= \int \text{TW\_Tput} \, (1 + \text{Growth}_{\text{Taiwan Transhipment @ HK}})^t \, (l_{TW}) \, (a_{TW}) \, dt$$

where,

(l_{ML}) represents various macro factors due to political and economic risks at TW, (a_{ML}) represents the impact of price premiums due to congestions at TW.

The significance of the three sets of causal factors is that intuitively, the domestically generated throughput for the Seaport of Hong Kong is expected to decline over time, largely attributable to the downsizing of the manufacturing sector in Hong Kong. In addition, Mainland China's generated throughput that is transhipped through Hong Kong is expected to decline over time, owing to the emergence of newer Seaports along China's Pearl River Delta region. Likewise, the transhipment cross-straits trade between Mainland China and Taiwan through Hong Kong is expected to decline over time, owing to the political uncertainty concerning the possible reunification between Mainland China and Taiwan.

These dynamic relationships can be envisaged as a system archetype that is in a "spiralling decline", a situation involving multiple reinforcing loops as depicted in Fig. 3.2. The inference is that in terms of policy design to reverse the decline and sustain growth in the throughput of the Seaport of Hong Kong, it is essential to plan that higher transhipment traffic be attracted from both Mainland China and Taiwan. Therefore, in contrast to the situation of a "spiralling decline", the reverse hypothesis of "spiralling growth" can be envisaged to be the appropriate basis for designing intervention policies to sustain the throughput growth of the Seaport of Hong Kong.

Fig. 3.2. "Spiralling Growth/Decline" System Archetype – Seaport of Hong Kong Throughput

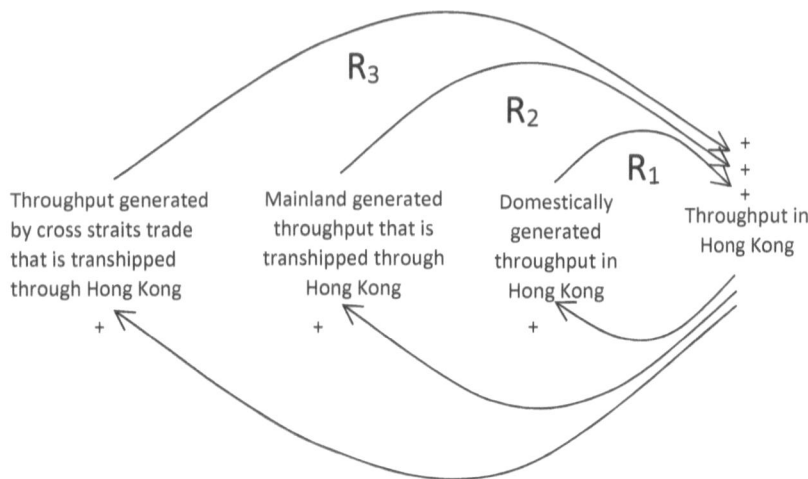

Source: Authors, 2020

However, there are two fundamental assumptions in the causal loop diagram of Fig 3.2. First, it is widely believed that the Seaport of Hong Kong's competitiveness vis-à-vis the Seaports in Mainland China stems not only from its operational efficiency, but also from a generally perceived higher degree of market transparency. As a consequence, although the seaport charges of the Seaport of Hong Kong are on the whole higher than those of the seaports of Mainland China, many shipping lines, shippers and consignees still prefer to use the Seaport of Hong Kong due to its overall cost effectiveness (HKPMB, 2001). Such an observed trend is expected to change over time.

With China's accession into the World Trade Organisation (WTO), there is a progressive rationalisation of customs procedures for the movement of goods and people between Hong Kong and Mainland China. A key consideration is concerned with Mainland China's technical competence in developing and operating seaports. Owing to the opening up of the China economy to foreign direct investments, China's seaports have benefited from bought-in state-of-the-art technologies and management know-how in operating seaports, evident for e.g. the introduction of foreign management expertise from several international seaport investment and management companies into various China seaports. Such befitting Cjina seaports include the instances of the Hutchison International Terminal (HIT) of Hong Kong in the Yantian Seaport and the Shanghai Seaport; the PSA Corporation (PSA) of Singapore in the Dalian Seaport and the Guangzhou Seaport; and the P&O (Pacific and Orient) Company in the Shekou Seaport. The HIT, PSA, and the P&O company are reckoned to be the world leaders of seaport ownership and management, attaining large scale economics and strategic competitive advantages in their networks of global seaport operations. Therefore, and over time, decisions as to which seaport to use would be solely based on economic and commercial considerations rather than on non-commercial considerations like transparency, efficiency and technical competence.

Another important consideration that affects the competitiveness of seaports is their connectivity. The connectivity of seaports is defined to be the frequency and comprehensiveness of shipping services that connect a particular seaport of interest to other seaports of the world. It is implicit that seaport competitiveness underpins seaport connectivity that in turn underpins competitiveness. Such inter-relationships can be depicted as a reinforcing loop in Fig 3.3. Nevertheless, Seaports cannot become competitive only until they have each attained comprehensive connectivity. It is similar to the "chicken and egg" situation that would only be broken with an external intervention of major significance like an injection of new and substantial investment inflow in net terms, the introduction of policy design, inclusive of regulatory initiatives.

Fig. 3.3. The Competitiveness and Connectivity Spiral.

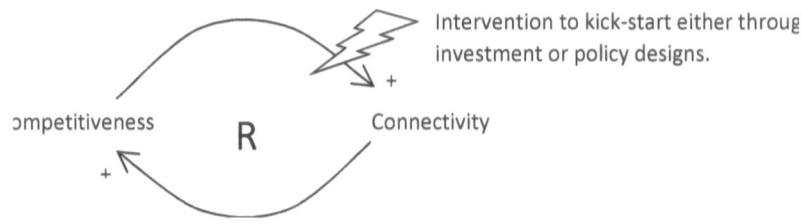

Source: Authors, 2020

Because of the twin factors of competitiveness and connectivity, the relationship between the Seaport of Hong Kong and China's Mainland seaports may well be based on either a competitive relationship or a complimentary relationship. However, the growth of the demand for seaport services in Mainland China would increase the overall market for seaports on Mainland China. Nevertheless, such demand growth would likely result in some spill over to the Seaport of Hong Kong, in the form of Mainland China's transhipment throughput through Hong Kong. Under such a scenario, the Seaport of Hong Kong enjoys improvements to its economies of scale and its connectivity. The ensuing growth of the Seaport of Hong Kong that acts to the detriment of the seaports of Mainland China would form the balancing loop to counteract the reinforcing loop for the growth for the seaports in Mainland China. These balancing and reinforcing loops are depicted as "B" and "R" respectively in Fig 3.4.

Fig 3.4. Complementary Versus Competitive Relationships Between the Seaport of Hong Kong and the Seaports in Mainland China

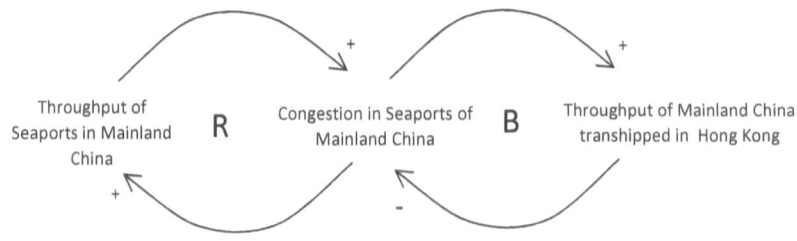

Source: Authors, 2020

Such countervailing force in Fig 3.4 may not be detrimental all the time. The spiralling growth of the seaports in Mainland China if left unchecked, may lead to an increase congestion that compromise trade to an extent that is destructive. Investments that would otherwise have gone into Mainland China may be diverted elsewhere. With the availability of an alternative gateway to Mainland China, through the Seaport of Hong Kong, the spill over to the Seaport of Hong Kong acts as a form of pressure release to prevent overheating in the Seaports in Mainland China. Therefore, the competitiveness of the Seaport of Hong Kong and the seaports in Mainland China can in fact complement each other. A more appropriate policy to drive the key relationship between the Seaport of Hong Kong and the seaports in Mainland China is needed to establish a sustainable equilibrium where the condition of complementary rather than competition would dominate.

In this regard, based on the principles of the market economy, the final 'arbiter' of this sustainable equilibrium would be the cost premium, associated with the use of the Seaport of Hong Kong, taking into consideration its higher productivity and cost effectiveness. In other words, for as long as the cost premium stays within a tolerable range, there would be some complementary effect in that the Seaport of Hong Kong and China's Mainland seaports can co-exist, and can grow the overall throughput pie to their mutual benefit. Conversely, once the cost premium of the Seaport of Hong Kong rises beyond a certain threshold, then the Hong Kong Seaport would not be able to sustain its relevance to Mainland China. The Seaport of Hong Kong would then lose a substantial part of its throughput to the seaports in Mainland China, particularly those along the Pearl River Delta. The Seaport of Hong Kong would have to solely depend on its domestic imports and exports to attract shipping lines to Hong Kong. However, as the shipment of physical goods to and from Hong Kong for domestic consumption, has been on the declining trend owing to an emphasis on services provision in preference to manufacturing. it is anticipated that in the extreme, the Seaport of Hong Kong may well relegate its role to largely that of a regional feeder Seaport.

The foregoing discussion brings Chapter 3's attention to focus on a key causal factor for the demand of seaport capacity i.e. the cost premium of the Seaport of Hong Kong. A relative index of seaport charges may well be constructed and be correlated to the throughput of the Seaport of Hong Kong, to form the supply curve of seaport capacity. With this supply curve, the threshold for the cost premium can be determined at that point where the slope of the seaport capacity supply curve changes substantially and eventually plateaus off. This cost premium seaport capacity relationship, as depicted in Fig 3,4, and can be likened to the "Stress-Strain" curve under the subject of material science. The "Throughput of the Seaport of Hong Kong" is analogous to "Stress". The "Seaport Costs" is analogous to "Strain" while the "cost premium" can only be applicable within the elastic range of the curve. The challenge to seaport planners and policy makers is therefore to make pricing and seaport expansion decisions such that the actual throughput would occur within an elastic range (Headlands, *et. al.* 2004).

The "stress-strain" curve for price premium i.e. in terms of the 'Terminal Handling Charges' (THC) with respect to the indigenous throughput and congestion within the Seaports of Hong Kong, Mainland China and Taiwan, has been dynamically modelled into the DPPM model as shown in Fig 3.7 subsequently

Fig. G 3, 5. Throughput Versus Cost Premium At The Seaport Of Hong Kong

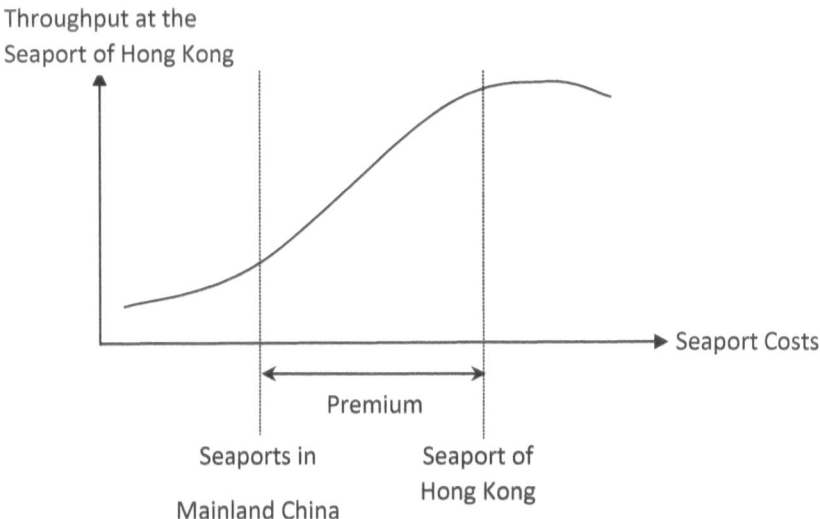

Source: Authors, 2020

In reality, the cost of seaport usage is not limited to seaport charges. There are other hidden costs to be taken into consideration owing to several reasons for e.g. congestion, delays, inefficiency, extended storage penalties, lack of transparency, potential breakage owing to double handling in the course of transhipment and discounts, The hidden costs and/or benefits are difficult to quantify and are unlikely to be available with high accuracy. Alternative levers that are objective and are available to policy makers to work with would have to be found. One of these alternatives would be in the form of a "Dampener", which acts in the same way as seaport charges that in turn act to check against the runaway throughput increases of the Seaport of Hong Kong. Such as "Dampener" can be effectively defined as:

$$\text{Dampener} = \text{Hong Kong\_Seaport\_Congestion} = \text{T'put}_{\text{Hong Kong}}(t) / \text{Capacity}_{\text{Hong Kong}} \quad (3.5)$$

Seaport congestion can be dealt with by either reducing the demand for seaport services or increasing the supply of seaport capacity. Based on the assumption that the Seaport of Hong Kong is generating returns to the seaport operating companies as well as to the economy of Hong Kong, that are at least comparable to other forms of investments or alternative uses of the associated land, direct real estate and physical infrastructure, then policy makers should seek to raise the supply of capacity rather than to drive away demand. They can so do by expanding the Seaport. Thus, the seaport expansionary policies would act like a "Pressure Release Valve" to ensure that seaport congestion is contained in a manner such that the cost premium would be applicable within the elastic range of the "Throughput versus Seaport Costs" curve. Furthermore, in terms of policy implementation, various mechanisms can be established like the timing to expand and the quantum of expansion (in terms of millions TEU per year) that can be triggered by the degree of seaport Congestion. The policy implementation mechanisms can be represented as multiple levels or as a nested set of "IF-THEN-ELSE" conditional statements:

Expansion Plan A: IF (β < Congestion <= $\beta + \delta_1$),
THEN (Implement Expansion Plan B),
ELSE (Consider the next condition); (3.6)

Expansion Plan B: IF ($\beta + \delta_1$ < Congestion <= $\beta + \delta_1 + \delta_2$),
THEN (Implement Expansion Plan C),
ELSE (Consider the next condition); etc. (3.7)

Expansion Plan C: IF ($\beta + \delta_1$ < Congestion <= $\beta + \delta_1 + \delta_2 + \delta_3$),
THEN (Implement Expansion Plan D),
ELSE (Consider the next condition); etc. (3.8)

Given that there would be congestion, the Seaport of Hong Kong throughput that is expressed by eq (3.1) previously would not be fully realisable. Indeed, there would be the inevitable dynamic interaction involving the multiple forces of the increase in demand, the building up of congestion or the "Dampener" as discussed earlier, and its subsequent moderation owing to expansion of seaport capacity. Therefore, the eventual realistic throughput of the Seaport of Hong Kong needs to be adjusted by the amount equivalent to that by the "Dampener". In recognition that in the actual situation, the short term responses tend to go through cycles of overloading (in this instance, throughput exceeding the capacity momentarily) and over correction (in this instance, some businesses being driven away by congestion and there will be a time lag before the business would return even if capacity was eventually expanded to cater to them). Thereafter, a sinusoidal function ξ may well have to be incorporated into the "Dampener". The dynamic interaction can be set in the following equations:

$$\text{T'put}_{\text{Hong Kong}} (t) (\text{Adjusted}) = \text{T'put}_{\text{Hong Kong}} (t) / \text{Dampener} \quad (3.9)$$
$$\text{Dampener} = \text{Seaport Congestion} + \xi (\text{Amplitude, Period}) \quad (3.10)$$

where,

Amplitude can be imputed with a constant σ multiplied by seaport congestion, and the period can be derived from the average tenure of the Terminal Services Agreements that shipping lines sign with the seaports.

Similar to the situation in which a significant part of the throughput owing to Mainland China is transhipped via the Seaport of Hong Kong, then a significant part of the China-Taiwan cross-straits throughput is also transhipped via the Seaport of Hong Kong. Therefore, in the DPPM modelling, the arguments and treatment with respect to transhipment throughput owing to Mainland China can be extended to the cross-straits throughput owing to Taiwan. In the prevailing absence of direct shipping between Taiwan and China, as there are no diplomatic and trade ties, then the Seaport of Hong Kong benefits from a major part to almost all of the transhipment trade between Taiwan and Mainland China. However, this beneficial situation may change if and when direct shipping between Taiwan and China becomes possible. Market forces would then redirect the extent of the cross-straits trade to transhipment through the Seaport of Hong Kong. While this transhipment is unfavourable to Taiwan and that the political union difficulty between China and Taiwan is a complex one that require a longer-term solution, the solution may well be a moderated growth projection for transhipment between Mainland China and Taiwan.

On the basis of the additional concepts of 'seaport congestion' and 'seaport expansion', the DPPM (dynamic seaport performance model) is appropriately refined with more causal loops as depicted in Fig 3.6.

Fig. 3. 6. A Refined Causal Loop Diagram for the Seaport of Hong Kong

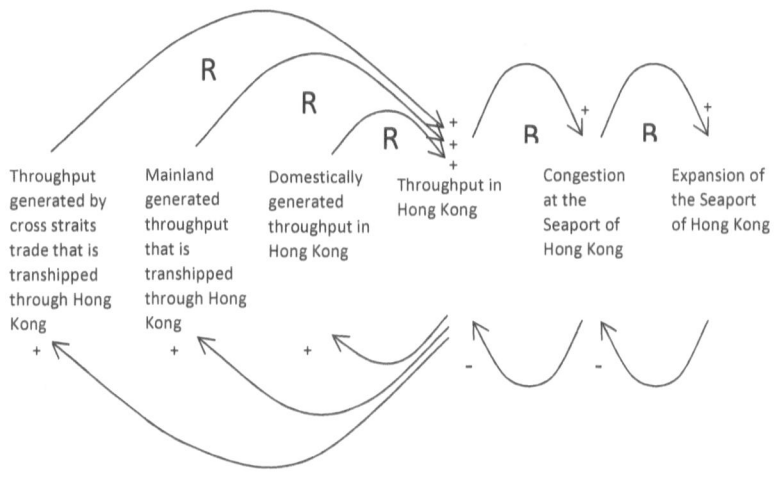

Source: Authors, 2020

The throughput growth rates of the Seaport of Hong Kong are modelled in eq (3.1) to eq (3.4) in terms of the numerical integration solution for a differential equation, with an annual time step that is adopted to minimize the integration error. The equation is solved by means of the Euler integration. Although the rates of change, i.e. the changes in Seaport throughput from year to year, may not remain constant, the results by way of the Euler integration are reasonable if the interval 'dt' is small and that the dynamics of the system are slow enough (Sterman, 2000). Nonetheless, if a higher order of integration accuracy is needed, then the Runge-Kutta numerical method can be considered. This is commonly deployed in the simulations of the physical system where the rules governing the rates, initial conditions, and parameters are known precisely and where small errors matter for this purpose.

THE MODEL ESTIMATION

Policy modelling, as in our DPPM examination is on the whole more concerned about the future and less about the past or the present but we can never really be certain about how the future unfolds, not even if we engage the DPPM with the best of intentions and the most thoughtful of policy designs (Bardach, 2000). It is through scenario analysis (sometimes known as scenario planning) and with the help of the DPPM that enable the painting of a realistic scenario for a preferred or a recommended policy alternative. This way, a comprehensive set of say 3 planned scenarios can be painted to enable us to take closer and realistic peeps into the possible future.

The final DPPM model is represented as a causal loop flow diagram in Fig 3.7 in terms of the stock and flow structures as well as the control and feedback structures. The flow diagram facilitates the simulation of the DPPM model under the syntax of an appropriate software for a period of ten years from the present (i.e. year t=10). This DPPM model can now be deployed for generating scenarios to support scenario planning and policy analysis, i.e. with respect to the particular interest of Chapter 3, that whether or not investments should continue to be poured into expanding the Seaport of Hong Kong, given that so many other seaports are emerging in China's Pearl River Delta region. Such seaport investments are analysed in two scenarios discussed below.

The question posed can be framed in a first scenario that attempts to see how the throughput of the Seaport of Hong Kong would perform if there is no further investment to expand its capacity, beyond the existing level of about 20 million TEU per year. The detailed conditions for this *ex ante* scenario are defined in the set of equations and presented in the computable program syntax, which is provided in Appendix I. The results of this *ex ante* first scenario are depicted in Fig 3.8 and Fig 3.9. Appendix II provides the results in further detail.

Fig. 3. 7 Causal Loop Flow Diagram of the DPPM For the Seaport of Hong Kong

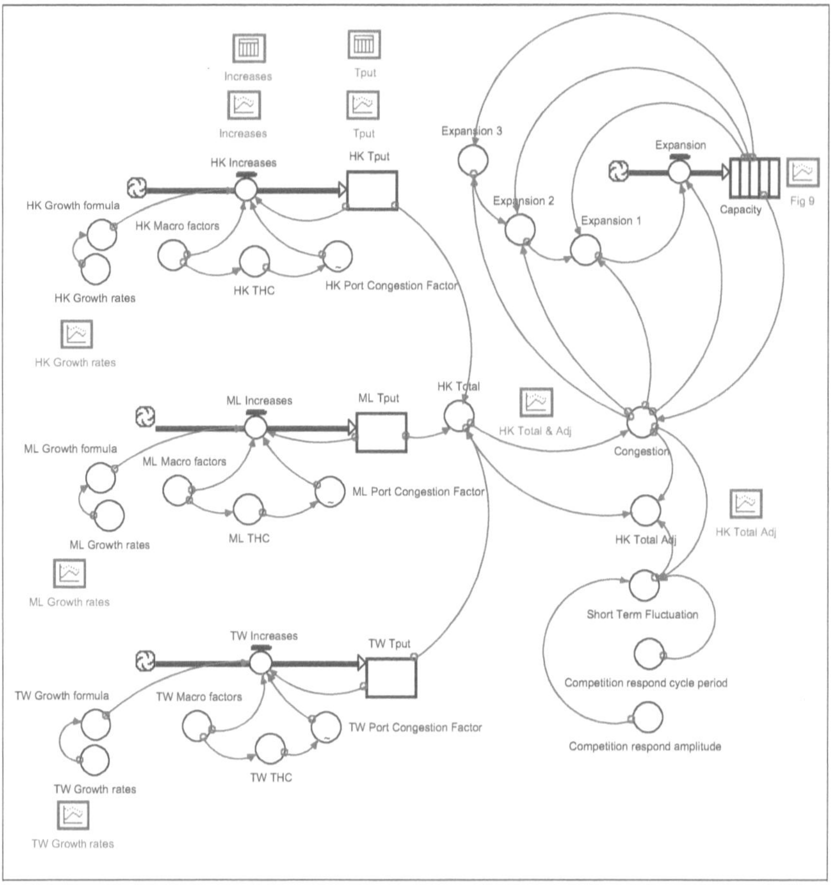

Source: Authors, 2020

Ex ante Scenario Analysés

Scenario 1: No Capacity Expansion

Fig 3.8 explicitly shows that without further and continued increase in seaport capacity under cenario 1, i.e. zero expansion throughout the period under examination, then the total throughput of the Seaport of Hong Kong would be capped by its capacity. As a result, and although there are potential increases in the throughput for Hong Kong (i.e. HK Total) as depicted along graph 4 of Fig 3.9, these opportunities could not be realised owing to capacity constraints. Similarly, potential increases in throughput without corresponding increases in capacity would only drive the "Hong Kong Seaport Congestion" upwards. If seaport management does not initiate measures to address the situation to facilitate throughput to increase beyond the existing Seaport capacity, then congestion and other costs would escalate up to its upper bound of the elastic limit. These congestion and other costs in turn would drive the actual seaport throughput back to a level equal to its capacity. Such cycles of deviation from the equilibrium position and subsequent corrections can be seen from the oscillations of graph 2 in Fig 3.8 around seaport capacity.

Fig 3.8. Scenario 1: No Capacity Expansion – Capacity, Expansion, Congestion, Throughput

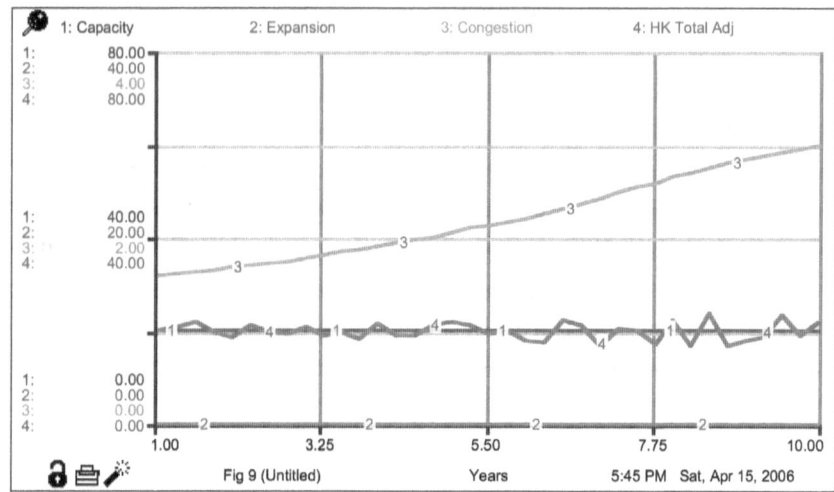

Source: ithink program, 2007; Authors, 2020

Fig 3.9. Scenario 1: No Capacity Expansion - Throughput

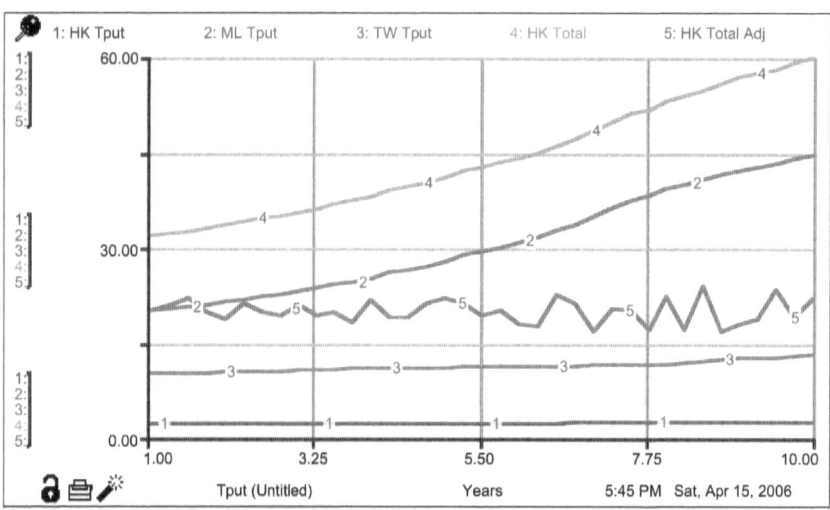

Source: ithink program, 2007; Authors, 2020

Scenario 2: Sustained capacity expansion

Contrary to the first scenario, Scenario 2 examines the effectiveness of supplying additional capacity in response to the rising demand for seaport services. In Scenario 2, the expansion of the capacity of the Seaport of Hong Kong is driven by the DPPM-guided policies i.e. seaport expansion would be implemented in conjunction with anticipated increase in throughput as well as seaport congestion level. The results of this *ex ante* Scenario 2 are depicted in Fig 3.10 and Fig 3.11. Appendix I provides the results in further detail.

Fig 3.10. Scenario 2: Continued Capacity Expansion – Capacity, Expansion, Congestion, Throughput

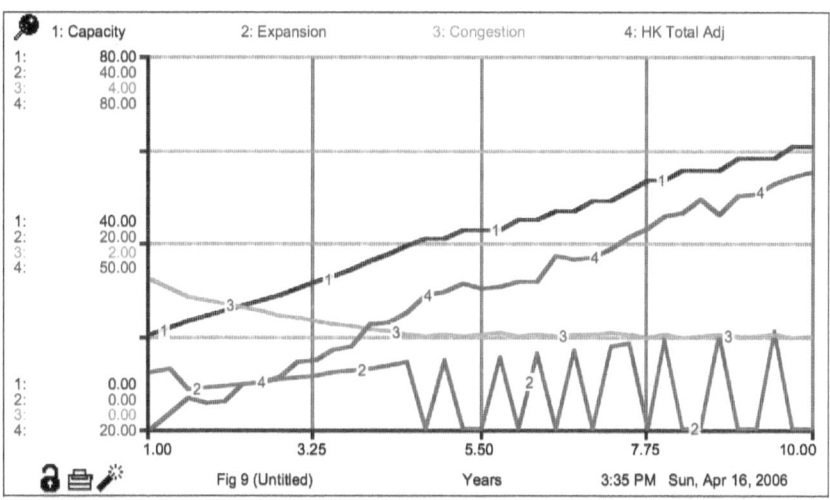

Source: ithink program, 2007; Authors, 2020

Fig 3.11. Scenario 2: Sustained Capacity Expansion – Throughput

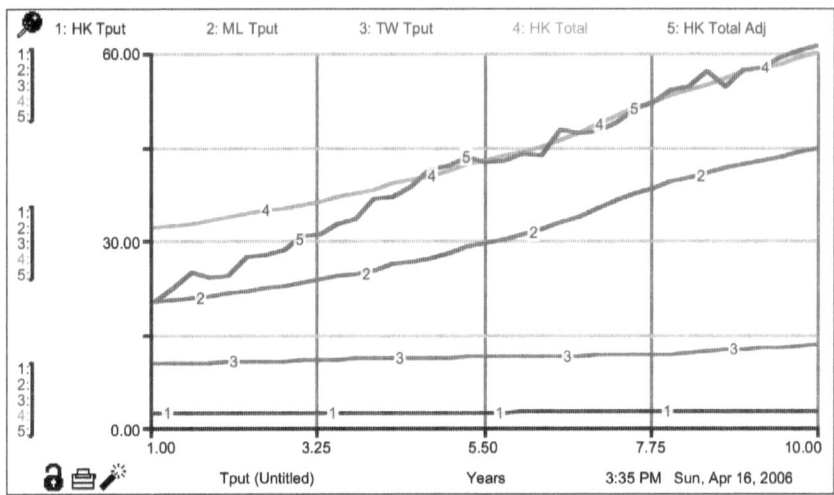

Source: ithink program, 2007; Authors, 2020

Graph 2 of Fig 3.10 shows the stepwise capacity expansions that are to be implemented in conjunction with increases in throughput. As a result, congestion is initially brought down to a manageable level and thereafter kept at that level with subsequent expansions executed in conjunction with the growth in demand. As a result, the throughput of the Seaport of Hong Kong would be able to continue to rise in conjunction with the rise in the demand and supply of additional capacity. This is depicted along graph 5 of Fig 3.11. In fact, the gradual closing of the gap between graphs 4 and 5 of Fig 3.11 shows how seaport expansion could be timed and executed in a manner that allows the Seaport of Hong Kong to optimise the opportunities of transhipment traffic from Mainland China and Taiwan.

Although the capacity expansions depicted along graph 2 of Fig 3.10 is computed to be in small incremental steps, it is unlikely that in the actual implementation of the expansion projects would be handled in such an incremental manner. It is because large infrastructure projects, like seaport expansion, are lumpy in nature in the sense that they have to be built and equipped in incremental steps of at least one berth at a time. This lumpy seaport expansion would yield a capacity increase of between 0.5 million to 1 million TEU per year, depending on the productivity as well as the quality and quantity of equipment used. Even then, to achieve the advantage of the economy of scale, the minimisation of disruption, and commercial viability, then seaport expansion projects are more likely to be implemented by building two or more berths at a time. In the case of Hong Kong where seaport ownership and management are privatised, this building of two or more berths at a time can be carried out by the awarding of concessions in packages of two or more berths at any one time. The most recent example is the award of the CT9 concessions to a joint venture amongst the major private seaport operators i.e. HIT, MTL and Cosco.

Scenario 3: Sensitivity Analysis – With Intermediate Level Of Capacity Expansion

Contrary to the scenarios 1 and 2, scenario 3 examines an intermediate strategy of offering some expansion that is lagging in apparent demand. Scenario 3 also serves to examine the sensitivity of how the throughput of the Seaport of Hong Kong may respond to capacity expansion. The results of this *ex ante* Scenario 3 are depicted in Fig 3.12 and Fig 3.13. Appendix I provides the results in further detail.

Fig 3.12. Scenario 3: Sensitivity analysis, with intermediate level of capacity expansion – Capacity, Expansion, Congestion, Throughput

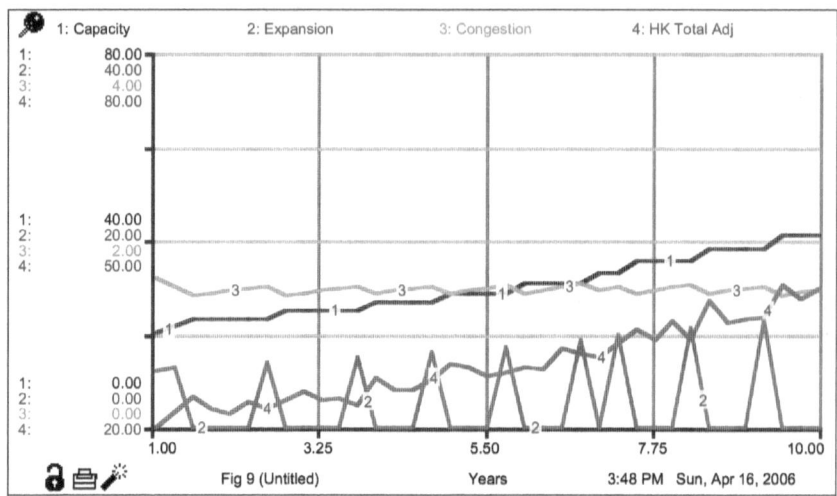

Source: ithink program, 2007; Authors, 2020

Fig 3.13. Scenario 3: Sensitivity Analysis, With Intermediate Level of Capacity Expansion –Throughput

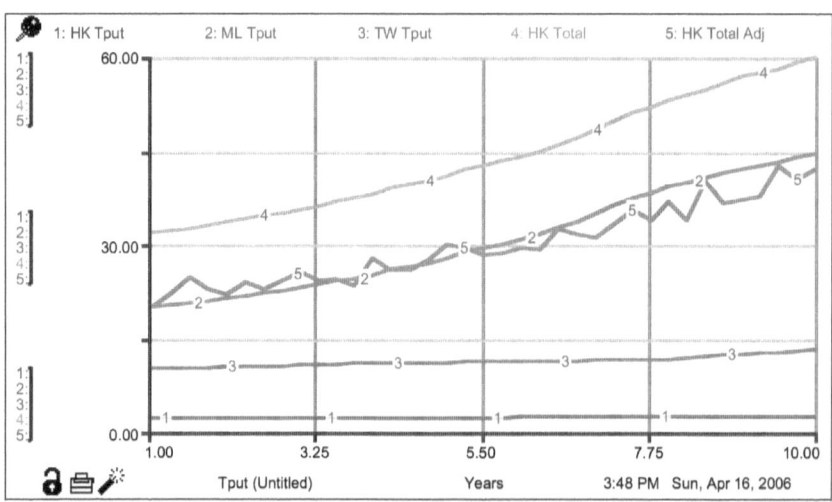

Source: ithink program, 2007; Authors, 2020

Graph 2 of Fig 3.12 depicts a relatively more modest approach towards capacity expansions when compared with Graph 2 of Fig 3.10. As a result, although congestion is checked, total throughput of the Seaport of Hong Kong after being adjusted due to congestion is also checked. In the case of scenario 2, the total throughput at year 10 is about 60 mil TEU/year, whereas in the case of scenario 3, it is about 40 mil TEU/year.

Another observation to highlight is that in scenario 2, in accordance with the strategy of supplying the expanded capacity in line with anticipated demand, the actual throughput at the Seaport of Hong Kong is able to 'catch-up and meet with demand. Such demand satisfaction can be seen in the closing of the gap between Graph 4 and Graph 5 of Fig 3.11. No such closing of gap occurs under scenario 3 as it the supply of capacity is never intended to 'catch up' with anticipated demand in full. Such capacity supply not to 'carch up' with anticipated demand can be observed when comparing Graph 4 and Graph 5 of Fig 3.13.

Concluding Remarks

Seaport capacity expansion can in effect be deemed to be an attractive, planned urban development policy for many seaports in the developing economies. From the direct real estate (DRE)perspective, Seaports are often invested and used like other large physical land infrastructure assets like highways to stimulate the economic development of a region or to promote the appreciation of DRE capital values (CVs) in the vicinity of seaports. It is believed that to some extent, the demand for physical land infrastructure or seaports is supply driven. As a consequence, competition between different regions of the same country or of competing economies in a particular region of the world have each intensified in recent years. Competition is also being fuelled as more and more seaports are being privatised in recent years.

However, without careful planning, the seaport capacity expansions may lead to financial difficulties in the long term, if the projected seaport throughput and revenue growth do not materialize.

In the context of urban planning and development, failed seaport development projects due to abandonment before completion, may well lead to the dereliction of land and worse still, urban degeneration associated with the growth of urban slums. As shown in Fig 3.14, the underutilization of seaports may necessitate a full or partial conversion of use as a symptomatic response to compensate the shortfall in earnings of the seaport (in the balancing loop B1). The result is the introduction of unintended and incompatible activities into an area originally zoned for seaport use (in the reinforcing R3). The further unintended side effects this may cause include the overloading of other urban infrastructure, the disruptions to the DRE values of the surrounding properties, and other impact on the environment (in reinforcing R4) (Amekudzi & Meyer, 2006). The unfavourable outcome may well be to further deter future investments like the logistics or industrial activities, which should have been the fundamental response to improve the seaport performance from coming in (balancing loop B2) (Campbell, 1996).

Fig 3.14. Implications of Failure of Seaport Projects

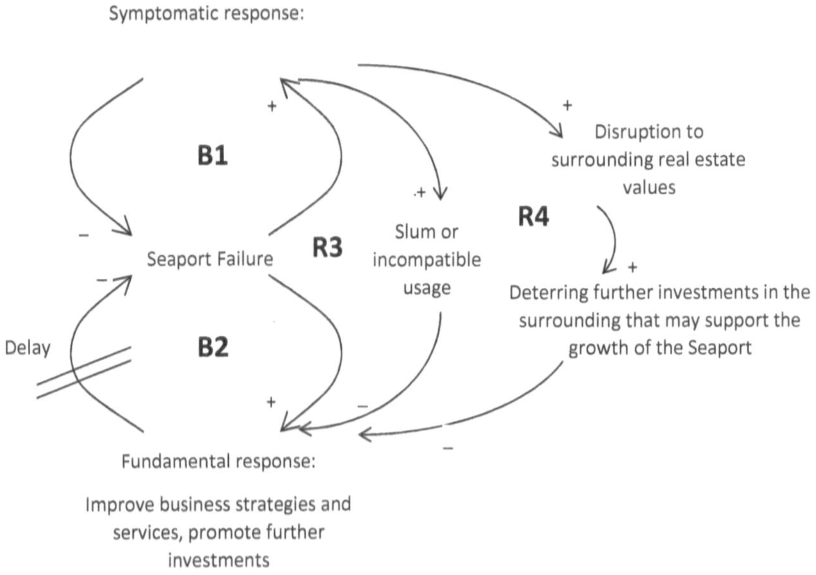

Source: Authors, 2020

Therefore, before any expansion is undertaken, due diligence has to be done in order to obtain a realistically anticipated future seaport throughput and profitability of the desired expansion (Kartwright, et. al. 2001). At the same time, care should also be taken to evaluate the opportunity costs, resulting from such land-use zoning, as the opportunity costs will have long term repercussions (Ben-Joseph, 2005).

In the case of the Seaport of Hong Kong, there are altogether eight seaports in its vicinity that are concurrently serving the same Pearl River Delta region. These seaports include the Guangzhou Seaport, Shekou Seaport, Chiwan Seaport, and the Yantian Seaport. Although these eight Seaports can act as a network to complement one another to grow the overall throughput pie for all to share more or less evenly, it is also possible that competition should result in some gaining more than the others. In particular, the Seaport of Hong Kong can be adversely affected most as its traditional role as a global transhipment hub for not only for Pearl River Delta region, but also for other parts of China can be diluted by the newer seaports emerging in China.

Chapter 3 has developed a rigorous and robust DPPM model on a reasonably sized and simplified scale. In particular, the DPPM is validated with scenarios 1 and 2 depicting the extremes of doing nothing and aggressively expanding to catch up with projected demand, which was projected at 60 mil TEU/year in 10 years' time. The robustness of the DPPM is also verified with a sensitivity test adopting scenario 3, which pursues a modest expansion strategy, thereby projecting a throughput at an intermediate level of 40 mil TEU/year in 10 years' time. Thus, the DPPM when extended to take a close look at the Seaport of Hong Kong, offers meaningful insights into how the Seaport of Hong Kong may well be able to respond to changing market conditions and emerging competition as well as to play a sustained role in the future.

The wide-ranging policy formula that has given the Seaport of Hong Kong great success in the past - i.e. good infrastructure, efficient operations, effective management, a free Seaport status, a well-defined legal system, well-established financial and business services, to name a few - should continue to offer the Hong Kong economy and its Seaport with a competitive edge. However, this policy formula is clearly not enough going forward, nor is it prudent for infrastructure planning and development in the Hong Kong and the neighbouring Shenzhen area to proceed in an uncoordinated manner. This approach may eventually lead to a destructive form of competition, to the detriment of all the parties concerned. Furthermore, it is also not desirable to have too many seaports within the same region without the supporting logistics ecosystem like warehousing, consolidation and distribution system, shipping connectivity, and other factors correspondingly addressed.

Instead, the entire Pearl River Delta including Hong Kong can be deemed to be an integrated region. While the Seaport of Hong Kong has been an established global transhipment hub for Mainland China as well as for other parts of Asia, the rest of the Pearl River Delta region can leverage on the opportunity to complement Hong Kong so that the whole region can be the logistics hub for China, and in particular the Southern region, which is beyond the catchments of Shanghai and the Yangtze Estuary (Fig 3.15). The complimentary activities can gravitate towards the Southern region, which in turn may well leverage on its own comparative advantage that Hong Kong does not have, namely, relatively cheap land, cheap labour as well as more competitive logistics, logistics related semi-manufacturing and manufacturing industries.

Fig 3.15. Seaport Of Hong Kong and the Seaports In Mainland China

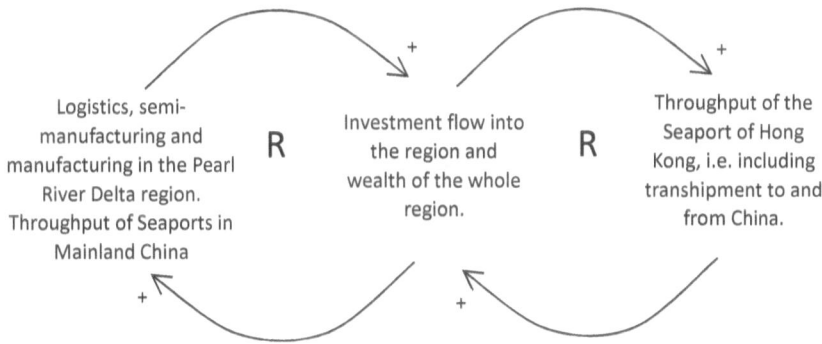

Source: Authors, 2020

On the basis of of the foregoing strategic considerations, the growth potential of the Seaport of Hong Kong as depicted in Scenario 2 can become a reality. Corresponding to the seaport capacity expansion plans derived from the DPPM analysis, efforts should also be put into ensuring that the movement of cargo, people, and trade information between Hong Kong and the rest of China's Pearl River Delta region be as seamless and cost-effective as possible. In this regard, it is noted that there have been initiatives from both the public and the private sectors to synergize for mutual benefit. For e.g. the formation of the Guangdong-Hong Kong Coordination Unit in the SAR (special administrative region) Government has stepped up the working meetings between the corresponding authorities in Shenzhen and Hong Kong; the commencement of a 24-hour full-scale boundary crossing; and other initiatives have demonstrated a much closer relationship being forged between the authorities in the SAR and the South China region. Other initiatives under study include the single operations for Customs inspection and clearance at the border, the co-location of the Hong Kong and Mainland Customs so that trucks need to stop only once, the development of a Freight Village and Green Pipelines, the greater use of advanced IT to speed up customs clearance, and the interfacing between Hong

Kong's Digital Trade & Transport Network and China's "electronic Seaport" system.

Chapter 3 begins with the investigation of the relationship between seaport throughput and capacity expansion. Subsequently, the DPPM is introduced as a rigorous alternative, which utilises the principles of system dynamics, to support *ex ante* scenario planning and policy analysis. It is hoped that Chapter 3 would provide planners, policy makers and investors a structured framework to examine possible questions and the appropriate policy decisions they would make. The DPPM can potentially be expanded to incorporate more factors and to deal with more complexities. It is hoped that the work of Chapter 3 would have provided a useful basis for further research in policy evaluation.

References

Amekudzi, Adjo A., Meyer, Michael D. (2006). "Considering the Environment in TransSeaportation Planning: Review of Emerging Paradigms and Practice in the United States." Journal of Urban Planning and Development. ASCE. Vol: 132(1). March, 2006.

Balling, Richard J., Taber, John T., Brown, Michael R., Day, Kirsten. (1999). "Multi-objective Urban Planning Using Genetic Algorithm." Journal of Urban Planning and Development. ASCE. Volume 125, Issue 2, pp. 86-99.

Ben-Joseph, Eran. (2005). "Innovating Regulations in Urban Planning and Development." Journal of Urban Planning and Development. ASCE. Volume 131(4).

Bardach, E. A Practical Guide for Policy Analysis. Chatham House Publishers, Seven Bridges Press, LLC, New York, 2000.

Business Times (23 Jul 2002). "Booming China Seaport sees more growth."

Business Times (26 Feb 2002). "Hong Kong remains world's busiest Seaport."

Campbell, Scott. (1996). "Green Cities, Growing Cities Just Cities?" Urban Planning and the Contradictions of Sustainable Development. Journal of the American Planning Association, Vol. 62.

Census and Statistics Department. (2001). Hong Kong Annual Digest of Statistics. Various issues. Hong Kong Government Printer, Hong Kong.

Census and Statistics Department. (2001). Hong Kong Monthly Digest of Statistics. Various issues. Hong Kong Government Printer, Hong Kong.

Census and Statistics Department (2000). Hong Kong Shipping Statistics. Various issues. Hong Kong Government Printer, Hong Kong.

Cheng, Leonard K. and Wong, Yue-Chim Richard (1997) Seaport Facilities and Container Handling Services: The Hong Kong Economic Policy Studies. City University of Hong Kong Press, Hong Kong.

Enright, Micheal J., Scott, Edith E., Dodwell, David. (1997). The Hong Kong Advantage. Oxford University Press, Hong Kong.

Forrester, J (1993). "*System Dynamics and Lessons of 35 Years*" In Systems-Based Approach to Policymaking edited by Kenyon B De Greene, Kluwer Academic Publishers, Norwell, MA.

Government Secretariat Lands & Works Branch. (1989). Seaport & Airport Development Strategy: Final Report. Hong Kong Government Printer, Hong Kong.

Ho, K H D (1996). The Seaport Economy. Singapore University Press.

Ho, M W (1995). "Seaports in Shenzhen and Hong Kong." Internal Chapter 3 of JTC Corporation Singapore.

Hong Kong Seaport and Maritime Board (2001). Hong Kong Seaport Cargo Forecasts. Various Issues. Hong Kong Government Printer, Hong Kong.

Hong Kong Seaport and Maritime Board (2001). Summary Statistics on Seaport Traffic in Hong Kong (as at December 2001). Hong Kong Government Printer, Hong Kong.

Hong Kong Trade Development Council (1 Feb 1997). Limited immediate impact on Hong Kong in direct shipping links between Mainland and Taiwan. www.tdctrade.com.

Hui, Eddie C. M., Seabrokke, William., Wong, Gordon K. C. (2004). "Forecasting Cargo Throughput for the Seaport of Hong Kong: Error Correction Model Approach". Journal of Urban Planning and Development. ASCE. Vol: 130(4). December, 2004.

Hutchinson Seaport Holdings. (2001). Yantian International Container Terminals. <http://www.hph.com.hk/business/Seaports/china/yict.htm>

Invest HK (10 Feb 2003). Shipping and Container Services. www.investhk.gov.hk.

Headland, J.; Ellis, W.; Thompson, L.; Breeman, P. "Balancing Seaport Planning: Demand, Capacity, Land, Cost, Environment and Uncertainty." Seaports 2004. ASCE Conference Proceedings.

Jeon, Christy Mihyeon, Amekudzi, Adjo A., Vanegas, Jorge. (2006). "Transportation System Sustainability Issues in High-, Middle-, and

Low-Income Economies: Case Studies from Georgia (U.S.), South Korea, Colombia, and Ghana." Journal of Urban Planning and Development. ASCE. Vol: 132(3). September, 2006.

Kartwright, K.; Cottrill, L.; Hamrick, G.; Nye, L.; Leue, M. "Seaport of Long Beach/Los Angeles Transportation Master Plan." Seaports 2001. ASCE Conference Proceedings.

Kia M.; Shayan E.; Ghotb F. "Investigation of Seaport capacity under a new approach by computer simulation." Computers and Industrial Engineering, Volume 42, 11 April 2002, pp. 533-540(8). Elsevier Science.

Kwok, Ben (2002). "Hutchison sells stakes to shipping lines as strategic investments." South China Morning Post, 16 April 2002.

Lee, Sau Heng (2001). "Container Seaport Begins to Show Crisis: A Solution Should be Devised Early." Hong Kong Economic Journal, 6 December 2001.

Loo, Becky P. Y., Chow S. Y. (2006). "Sustainable Urban Transportation: Concepts, Policies, and Methodologies." Journal of Urban Planning and Development. ASCE. Vol: 132(2). June 2006.

National Bureau of Statistics of China (2001). China Statistical Yearbook, 2001. China: National Bureau of Statistics of China.

Ngai, Lup Chee and Lin, Katherine Pui Kar (1997). "The Development of Seaport Facilities in Hong Kong and Southern China." 6th Asia Pacific Sea Transport Conference, pp. 94-99.

Ogden, Jon (2002). "Wu slams Seaport bureaucracy." South China Morning Post, 12 March 2002.

Planning Department and Seaport and Maritime Board (2001). Seaport Development Strategy Review. Various Issues. Hong Kong Government Printer, Hong Kong.

Seaport and Maritime Board (2001). Seaport Development Strategy Review. Hong Kong Government Printer, Hong Kong.

Porter, Michael E (1990) The Competitive Advantage of Nations. Free Press, New York.

Richarson, G. (1985). Introduction to the system dynamics review. Syst. Dyn. Rev., 1(1), 1-5.

Richmond, B. (1991). Systems Thinking – Four Key Questions. High Performance Systems Inc.

Rotterdam Municipal Seaport Management (2000). Seaport Statistics 2000.

Seabrooke W. Hui, C.M. Eddie, Lam H.K. and Wong G.K.C. (2003). "Forecasting Cargo Growth and Regional Role of the Seaport of Hong Kong". Cities, 20 (1), 51-64.

Statistical Bureau of Guangdong. (2001). Guangdong Statistical Yearbook, 2001. China Statistics Press, China.

Sterman, J. (2000). Business dynamics: System thinking and modelling for a complex world. McGraw-Hill. New York.

Tung, Chee Hwa. (2001). Policy Address 2001.

Wang, James Jixian (1998) "The Formation of Hong Kong-Shenzhen Container Load Centre. Researches on Shipping Market and Management" Proceeding of International Conference on Shipping and Shipping Market Facing 21 Century, pp. 46-53.

World Trade Organization. (2001). International Trade Statistics 2001.

Yuen, Ming-Fai Richard (2001). "Future Development of Seaport of Hong Kong." In: Yeh, Gar-On Anthony, Hills, Peter R, and Ng, Ka-Wing Simon, (Eds), Modern Transport in Hong Kong for the 21st Century. Centre of Urban Planning and Environmental Management, University of Hong Kong, Hong Kong, pp.49-59.

Appendix I : Results in tables

Table 1. Scenario 1 - No capacity expansion

	HK Tput	ML Tput	TW Tput	HK Total	Capacity	Congestion	Expansion	HK Total Adj
Initial	2	20	10	32	20	1.6		20
1	2.03	21.44	10.26	33.74	20	1.69	0	18.67
2	2.06	23.03	10.55	35.64	20	1.78	0	20.97
3	2.09	25.13	10.93	38.15	20	1.91	0	21.65
4	2.14	27.91	11.07	41.13	20	2.06	0	22.12
5	2.19	30.77	11.21	44.17	20	2.21	0	17.97
6	2.23	35.08	11.42	48.73	20	2.44	0	16.73
7	2.28	39.54	11.61	53.42	20	2.67	0	22.45
8	2.33	42.38	12.49	57.19	20	2.86	0	17.95
9	2.37	44.68	13.15	60.21	20	3.01	0	21.98

Table 2. Scenario 2: Sustained capacity expansion

	HK Tput	ML Tput	TW Tput	HK Total	Capacity	Congestion	Expansion	HK Total Adj
Initial	2	20	10	32	20	1.6		20
1	2.03	21.44	10.26	33.74	25.24	1.34	5.24	24.18
2	2.07	23.03	10.54	35.64	30.1	1.18	4.86	30.74
3	2.11	25.13	10.91	38.16	35.89	1.06	5.79	36.81
4	2.16	27.91	11.06	41.13	40.96	1	5.07	41.99
5	2.22	30.77	11.2	44.19	44.73	0.99	3.77	43.82
6	2.27	35.08	11.4	48.75	48.85	1	4.12	47.51
7	2.32	39.54	11.58	53.45	53.34	1	4.49	54.26
8	2.38	42.38	12.45	57.21	58.25	0.98	4.91	57.55
9	2.43	44.68	13.1	60.22	60.87	0.99	2.62	61.52

Table 3. Scenario 3: Sensitivity analysis

	HK Tput	ML Tput	TW Tput	HK Total	Capacity	Congestion	Expansion	HK Total Adj
Initial	2	20	10	32	20	1.6		20
1	2.03	21.44	10.26	33.74	23.11	1.46	3.11	21.96
2	2.07	23.03	10.54	35.64	24.85	1.43	1.73	25.62
3	2.11	25.13	10.91	38.16	26.71	1.43	1.86	27.94
4	2.16	27.91	11.06	41.13	28.71	1.43	2	30.19
5	2.22	30.77	11.2	44.19	30.87	1.43	2.15	29.55
6	2.27	35.08	11.4	48.75	33.18	1.47	2.31	31.21
7	2.32	39.54	11.58	53.45	35.67	1.5	2.49	37.04
8	2.38	42.38	12.45	57.21	38.34	1.49	2.68	37.28
9	2.43	44.68	13.1	60.22	41.22	1.46	2.88	42.18

Appendix II : List of parameters

l_{HK} = Macro factors due to political and economic risks at Hong Kong.

a_{HK} = Price premium factor due to congestions at Hong Kong arising from indigenous demand.

l_{ML} = Macro factors due to political and economic risks at Mainland.

a_{ML} = Price premium factor due to congestions at Mainland arising from indigenous demand.

l_{TW} = Macro factors due to political and economic risks at Taiwan.

a_{TW} = Price premium factor due to congestions at Taiwan arising from indigenous demand.

Hong Kong_Seaport_Congestion Factor = $T'put_{Hong\ Kong}(t)$ / $Capacity_{Hong\ Kong}$.

ξ (Amplitude, Period) = Short term sinusoidal fluctuations due to inelasticity of demand and time lag to response to capacity expansion. Amplitude is with a constant σ multiplied by the Seaport Congestion, and Period can be derived from the average tenure of the Terminal Services Agreements shipping lines sign with Seaports.

HK_Growth_formula = Compounded growth of the Seaport of Hong Kong.
ML_Growth_formula = Compounded growth of the Seaports in Mainland.
TW_Growth_formula = Compounded growth of the Seaports in Taiwan.

HK Tput = Throughput at the Seaport of Hong Kong at Year 0.
ML Tput = Throughput at the Seaports in Mainland at Year 0.
TW Tput = Throughput at the Seaports in Taiwan at Year 0.

CHAPTER 4

THE GLOBAL OUTREACH OF THE PORT OF SINGAPORE PIVOTAL AND ITS MODEST ORIGIN

Chapter 4 is concerned with the global outreach of the small island state of Singapore's seaport operation, owing to its limited land area of a mere 724 sq. km (280 sq. miles) and its small population size of about 5.7 million by 2019 (according to the Department of Statistics, Ministry of Trade & Industry, Singapore). Such vital limiting considerations constrain Singapore's seaport available cargo throughput. To overcome this small island state's limiting growth prospects, it is essential to grow and sustain the global outreach of the Port of Singapore. Even sea transport remains a principal and popular means of reaching the British Isles, in conjunction with the availability of air travel and ready access via the tunnel across the English Channel to and from Europe. Owing to the foregoing circumstances, maritime trade and naval power have been important aspects of the rapid and full development of the Singapore and British economies and their statures globally. In fact, it would not be an exaggeration to say that Britain has to a major extent shaped the maritime world, and that of the major trade routes of the world. A case in point is observed in some of the British trading posts that have grown to become major seaports and economies of the world, notably Singapore and Hong Kong that emerge to be the top two most busy seaports globally for many years even before Shanghai, China's commercial centre, surpassed them in the twenty-first century.

Impact of the British-Singaporean Friendship in the Maritime World

Before the Europeans started to come to Southeast (SE) Asian region to trade, Singapore has already turned to become a popular seaport in the southern part of the Straits of Malacca, serving ships and traders in the region, and so connecting Singapore with other seaports along the Straits of Malacca like Jambi, Palembang and Kedah. However, in the 15th century, the Sultanate of Malacca had emerged to become a significant trading port. Correspondingly, Singapore experienced a decline in its importance as a trading seaport for the region.

Figure 1. Sir Stamford Raffles

Sir Stamford Raffles arrived at the Far East when the Dutch is the dominant power in SE East Asia well before free trade was open with China while settlements in Australia have yet to become a substantive economic system. Raffles formally hoist the British flag in Singapore on 29 January 1819. History has shown that such a founding of Singapore marks the resurgence of Singapore to become a major Asian seaport. Beyond securing access to the Straits of Malacca, Raffles dud assess that due to its geographical position, Singapore would be a centre of vast importance to commerce and trade. It has safe anchorage for all seasons and that Singapore is not too far from China, the Malayan Peninsula, Indian Continent, and the surrounding islands. In time to come, Singapore would grow to become the de-facto commercial capital of British Malaya in the late 19th and early 20th centuries. Roads and railways are built for commodities transportation like crude oil, rubber and tin from Malaya to Singapore, to be then shipped to Britain and other international markets. Therefore, Singapore has all the ingredients to be an emporium of British commerce and a fulcrum, from which Britain is well poised to extend its political influence beyond India. Thereafter, to secure Britain's access to trade with the SE and North East Asian regions. Due to Singapore's immense strategic importance, it did become the largest British base in the East and in South East Asia, even larger than Britain's presence in Hong Kong or anywhere in India.

Following Singapore's independence in 1965, Singapore has continued to grow its seaport organically at Keppel and subsequently at Tanjong Pagar, then at Pulau Brani, Pasir Panjang, Jurong, and Tuas. In terms of business strategy, Singapore has expanded from basic entrepot trade to developing an export-oriented economy the basis of value-added manufacturing and services. Two centuries after Raffles founding of British Singapore, Singapore has surpassed British sea ports in terms of size and sophistication, and it expanded to become a bona-fide international maritime hub, and to be one of the world's busiest seaport in its own right. The Port of Singapore has seaport facilities that are ultra-modern and rival those anywhere in the developed world. Indeed, the vision of Raffles is yet to fully unfold.

Framework for Strategic Maritime Collaboration (FSMC)

In spite of the progress made, one has to be circumspect that the picture was not a rosy one all the time. During the Second World War, Britain did position Singapore as the fortress that would play the role of the 'Gibraltar of the East' to defend its interest in Asia. Accordingly, Singapore is even equipped with the largest dry dock in the world at that time. Nonetheless, fortress Singapore did succumb to invading Japanese armed forces. After the Second World War, Britain had to review its strategic posturing in SE Asia. In spite of the strategic merits that Singapore did offer Britain, since the days of Raffles, a decision is taken eventually in 1968 to withdraw British forces each of the Suez Canal and to withdraw British bases from Singapore. Thereafter, another half a century did pass in time.

Many new trends in the economic and geo-political spheres have since emerged. Moving forward into the new post war world order, it would be wise for Britain and Singapore to put into perspective the lessons from the past and to think through strategically how they can leverage on the positive legacy of Britain's maritime prowess and their colonial friendship, to advance their common strategic interest. The shared concern then is enduring world peace and harmony. Therefore, the 'Framework for Strategic Maritime Collaboration' that is shown in Fig 4.2 offers much needed guidance to develop mutually beneficial strategies, which may help to sustain the advantageous partnership between Singapore and Britain in the next 200 years.

It is widely accepted that over 90% of the world's trade is seaborne and it is by far the most cost-effective way to move a lot of traded goods, raw materials and services globally. Whilst both Singapore and Britain continue to have great ambitions to continue to be world class seaport and maritime players, their success would be shaped by various crucial factors as highlighted in the Framework. Both Britain and Singapore face some similar challenges and constraint. Britain is many times larger than Singapore but can still be regarded as relatively small and similar to Singapore, in the sense that they both cannot rely on their domestic markets to support the growth of their seaport and maritime industries. Both countries are outward orientated in their trade, investment and services outlook each. They have to venture globally and be to highly and specifically relevant to the needs of their global customers. Both their economies are at the tertiary level where their cost of labour and other factors of production are high, relative to those available in the emerging economies. Therefore, Singapore and Britain have to compete to add-value to the realm of technology, innovation and service creativities. For example, and instead of just building larger or mega container ships, shipyards in Singapore have niched on building specialised vessels and oil-rigs for the oil and gas industry. Likewise, and instead of competing on size alone, seaports in Britain and Singapore would have to compete on efficiency, productivity, safety, reliability, and the comprehensiveness of supporting business services.

Fig. 4 2. Strategic Framework of Collaboration

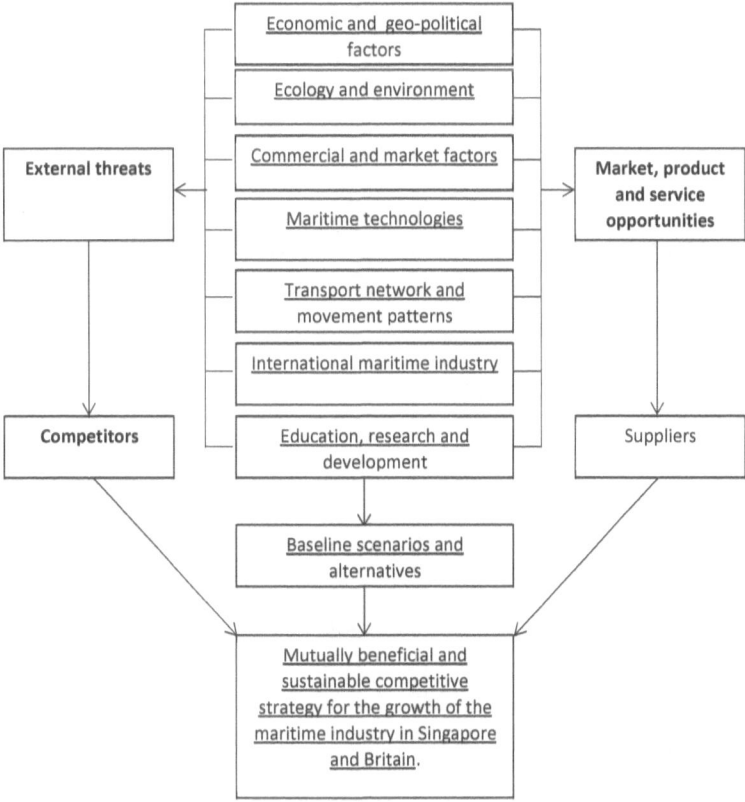

Source: Authors, 2020

At the education front, Singapore and Britain have recently rejuvenated their long history of collaborations. As Britain provided the earlier expertise for the design, construction, and operation of seaports, and shipping related matters, Britain contributed the bulk of what is now the body of knowledge for such matters. For example, ths city of Newcastle is one of the major ship-building centres in Britain. Accordingly, it was one of the pioneers of the discipline of naval architecture. When Singapore wanted to start a naval architecture programme, instead of creating one from scratch, it collaborates with the University of Newcastle to introduce such a programme at the Singapore Institute of Technology(SIT). Hopefully, such an initiative prompts various other research and development endeavours in engineering, high technology, information technology, trade analysis, seaport policy and other policy compact as well as in various other areas in years to come, to the benefit of nurturing strategic manpower to fuel the growth of the foregoing endeavours.

Beside universities, there are also many British firms that offer consulting services, be it in engineering, trade studies, etc. One such firm is the BMT Group, which was formed in 1985 from the former 'British Ship Research Association' and the 'National Maritime Institute'. Such a specialist engineering and technology firm in maritime transport, ports and in the oil cum gas sector, has participated in the master plan development for Singapore's Jurong Port in the Jurong industrial heartland, when Jurong Port then becomes a corporatized industrial port, hived off from its Jurong Town Corporation (JTC) parent in 2001. Yet another example is the 'Ocean Shipping Consultants' of the 'Royal Haskoning DHV'. This 'Ocean Shipping Consultants' form a specialist unit focusses on maritime economics and markets, offering a wide range of specialist due diligence and advisory services to support the maritime, seaports and logistics industries globally. Such a consultancy specialist unit's market research is also relied upon by the Singapore shipping community, private and public seaport policy makers to guide policy and strategy development.

British firms have leveraged on Singapore and can continue to deploy Singapore as their base and headquartered therein, to reach out to the vast Asian market. A key example is 'Castrol Ltd', who later became part of the 'British Petroleum (BP) group. Castrol is a long-standing British brand in the lube (i.e. lubricant) oil business. It originally had a plant at Singapore's Hill View area in the middle of Singapore. When the then Hill View land area was is acquired by the Singapore government for redevelopment in the late 1990s, Castrol explored its options to relocate to other parts of SE Asia but eventually chose to reinvest in Singapore, with a facility at Jurong Port. The continued engagement of Castrol in Singapore is a prime example of BP's successful operations in Singapore for over 50 years in businesses that include oil, gas, chemicals, carbon and business financing. Indeed, Singapore is BP's regional headquarters for shipping, consumer lubricants, industrial lubricants, marine fuel, marine lubricants and aviation fuels.

Indeed, many developing countries in the Asian region and other parts of the world are on the threshold of requiring massive investments in large scale and complex physical infrastructure. Therefore, British and Singaporean firms can so complement each other to venture into such a new and large physical infrastructure investment market. Collectively, the expertise can be put together to include not only the design, development and operation of physical infrastructure, but to also help structure commercial deals with their combined legal expertise, technical know-how and financial resources.

At the governmental level, Britain and Singapore can continue to work together in global platforms to help the global maritime community develop institutions and improve governance frameworks, so as to advance the good order of global maritime practices. One of which is the International Maritime Organization (IMO), which has its headquarters in London, and with whom Singapore is privileged to be an IMO council member since 1993. Such multi-lateral engagements of the global maritime community are increasingly needed as the world is experiencing more risks of conflicts as globalization deepens. With the continuous strengthening of the international maritime, shipping and trade law and with better transparency in place, everyone in the global community would stand to benefit from the certainty offered by such institutions and governance frameworks.

Concluding Remarks

The late Sir Stamford Raffles, with great strategic foresight, took possession of the then unimportant and insignificant island state of Singapore. He envisaged that Singapore would become a significant trading port that would well serve the interests of Britain. His vision has largely panned out to be true. Today, Singapore is no longer a colony of Britain. Singapore is an interdependent sovereign island state. Britain is no longer a colonial master. Yet, both countries remain close friends and strategic partners whereby their future relationship would continue to be founded on their historical bond and shaped by the alignment of their strategic interests in the global new order. Indeed, the British maritime legacy in Singapore should not be confined to some maritime museums. Such a legacy should be leveraged upon as the basis to create value and improve the lives the peoples of both countries and globally. There is tremendous scope for public and private sectors' participation from both countries to form strategic and business alliances, based on the vision and the meaningful of the 'Framework for Strategic Maritime Collaboration'.

CHAPTER 5

THE AIRPORT ECONOMY – THE SINGAPORE CHALLENGE

Airports play a significant role in the modern world. In the increasingly globalized world, aviation connects countries and cities via their airports. The airport fosters economic activities by encouraging international trade and tourism to facilitate the ease and speed of movement of cargoes and people. In general, airports support employment creation. For a start, the development of airports, which are usually massive undertakings that would span a number of years would create direct employment opportunities whereby workers and professionals in the direct real estate and construction sectors are deployed to design and build airports. When airports become operational, there would be the need for a lot of manpower to operate and maintain them. Airports crucially need manpower for their essential activities like air traffic management, aircraft maintenance, passenger services, cargo services, airport maintenance, storage and distribution of air fuels, security services, immigration and customs services to name several.

Airports offer increased accessibility which would in turn fuel the growth of the global tourism industry. In fact, global tourism accounts for some 30% of the world's trade of services, and 6% of the overall exports of goods and services. With an increase in the number of visitors and airport users, more money would flow into the local economy. The result in is sustainable and robust rising economic activities, employment and consumer behavioural changes, all of which should readily raise the standard of living of the population. Singapore is expected to substantially attract as many as about 16 million visitor arrivals in the mid-2000s and thereafter such visitor arrivals would sharply rise to about 40 million in that order of magnitude. There is potentially a vast visitor-arrivals market to tap on and grow robustly.

Since the founding of modern-day Singapore by the Briton Sir Stamford Raffles in 1819, Singapore has fast expanded to become the major gateway city in Asia to the rest of the region, Europe and the Americas. Indeed, and with the deepening growth of the global aviation industry, Singapore's airport development has taken on a similar growth trajectory. Reflecting on how airport designs have immensely changed over the years, one can observe the due influence of nation building priorities on Singapore's airport development. Singapore's first civilian airport was the Kallang Airport, which was opened in 1937. The modest Kallang airport has a circular landing ground that enabled air planes to land from or take off into any direction. The airport at Kallang district did also have a slipway to cater to flying boats. Subsequently, Kallang Airport outgrew its size and was made obsolete due owing to the rapid advancement in high technology aviation hat have accommodated larger, heavier and more complex aircrafts. There had been insufficient land space soon enough to expand Kallang Airport and any such expansion would need to encroach conflictingly into the well-established residential and commercial neighbouring suburb of Geylang. The proposed expansion of Kallang Airport had been found to be not feasible and dropped. A new site would need to be found to build a new airport. Initially, the Public Works Department (PWD) had identified Changi district but was not chosen because results from soil investigations indicate that the bearing capacity of the subsoil is insufficient. It would be too costly an undertaking to strengthen the Changi subsoil. The Tengah, district has been used as a British Air Base (and subsequently as a Republic of Singapore Air Force base, RSAF) had been considered, but deemed too small to be expanded into a civilian airport. Finally, the choice is the Paya Lebar district in 1950, located about 8 km north east of the Singapore town centre, and would be the site of the new civilian airport. The old Kallang Airport did effectively serve daily flights between Kallang Airport and Malaysia's airports of Kuala Lumpur, Ipoh and Penang.

However, high and teeming air traffic led to Kallang Airport's closure in 1955. The replacement is then the Paya Lebar Airport while the government's People's Association (PA) used the main building of the former Kallang Airport as the PA headquarters from 1960 till 2009. Although Kallang Airport did operate for only a short period from 1937 to 1955, the Airport had hosted the visits of many foreign dignitaries like Mr Richard M. Nixon, then Vice President of the United States of America (US), and his wife on 26 October 1953.

Paya Lebar Airport did develop its required facilities and commenced operations in 1955. However, by the early 1970s, it had become apparent that it too would be reaching its maximum capacity. The passenger traffic did rise sharply from 300,000 visitor arrivals in 1955 to 1.7 million in 1970 and 4 million in 1975 visitor arrivals respectively. Therefore, a decision would need to be made to either expand the Paya Lebar Airport or to build a new airport at another location. A consultant engaged by the government had recommended the Paya Lebar Airport to be expanded with a second runway and with additional passenger terminals. However, there did remain concerns that the Paya Lebar Airport is located in an area bounded by other large and complex mixed-use urban developments on all sides. It would therefore not be possible to expand the Paya Lebar Airport beyond two runways should the need arise in the future.

Even if the passenger handling capacity at the Paya Lebar Airport is adequate, aircrafts approaching or departing from the Paya Lebar Airport would have to fly over urban public and private housing, commercial and industrial concentrations, together with large and very dense population clusters in the vicinity. Heavy air traffic would not only cause severe noise, exhaust fumes and dust pollution for years to come, but also limit the scope of urban development owing to height restrictions and noise reduction measures that need to be imposed on buildings under the flight paths. For chronic and severe land scarce Singapore that also needs to intensify its land use by building taller buildings, the challenges to resolve land scarcity, urban development rules, restrictions and control measures warrant creativity innovation and artfulness to attain non-conflicting land uses. Land and direct real estate users can live, work, shop and play in steady-state peace, team work and harmony.

Contrary to the recommendations of consultants, the government had taken the bold and sound decision in 1975 to build a new global airport at the site of the RSAF Changi Air Base, to be augmented with substantial foreshore land reclamation from the sea. Thereafter, and in time come, Singapore started its journey *en route* to form and nurture the 'Global Changi Airport Hub', to al intents and purposes. It is then common sight to encounter at the Changi site complex the teeming flow of passenger traffic, boarding global flights like Singapore Airline (SIA)'s global flights between Singapore and the rest of the world, and vice versa. Despite such a successful journey, it is noteworthy that the journey remains unabated post the historic 1972 separation of the former amalgamated Malaysia Singapore Airlines (MSA). into two distinctly separated entities of the Malaysia Airlines System (MAS) and Singapore Airlines (SIA). Another memorable occasion of the warm handshake between Mr Lee Kuan Yew, Prime minister of Singapore and Chin's paramount leader, Mr Deng Xiaoping, who did arrive at Singapore's former Paya Lebar Airport on 12 November 1978, for an official three-day visit as vice-premier of China.

Whilst both Singapore's Kallang Airport and Paya Lebar Airport had been designed primarily for their functionality as a facility for aviation to meet their immediate needs then, the decision to build the Changi airport was to become a game changing occasion. For a start, planes approaching or departing Changi Airport would be flying over the sea, to avoid the issue of noise pollution like that for the Paya Lebar Airport. Accordingly, Changi Airport would provide the scope and flexibility of unrestrained 24-hour operations. The approach flight path of Changi Airport over the sea should help to avoid disastrous consequences on the ground in the event of an air mishap. The key strength of the Changi site for the new airport is that it can be further expanded with more foreshore land reclamation from the sea. From the initial two runways, provisions are made for a further two runways to be added in future. The runways are configured with sufficient separation from one another so that simultaneous aircraft take-off or landing can take place on each of them. Indeed, the recent decision to expand Changi Airport with a third runway and Terminal 5 would not be possible had the airport remained at Paya Lebar. With the opening of Changi Airport in 1981, the airport in Paya Lebar was subsequently converted for military use as the RSAF Paya Lebar Air Base. Crowd at the official opening of Singapore's S$ billion Changi Airport had been officially opened at a special reception, and with Defence Minister Howe Yoon Chong guest of honour, who had mentioned the air travel boom to come. Mr Howe is remembered as the man, who advocated the shift from the former Paya Lebar Airport to Changi Airport.

The hard work of building Changi Airport has been paying off. Changi Airport is a top airport in terms of customer service and security. It has won over 390 awards and accolades as the best global airport since its opening in 1981, from organisations like Skytrax and Business Traveller. Correspondingly, the evidence from the business outcome is encouraging as evident from the spike in volume of passenger traffic, airfreight and aircraft movements of Table 5.1. Singapore's global Changi Airport has become a standard bearer that offer the impetus to regional competitors to subsequently redevelop or expand their respective airports, namely Malaysia's airports of Kuala Lumpur, those of Bangkok and Hong Kong.

Table 5.1. Volume of Passenger, Airfreight and Aircraft Movements

Year	Passenger	Airfreight (tonnes)	Aircraft movements
1998	23,803,180	1,283,660	165,242
1999	26,064,645	1,500,393	165,961
2000	28,618,200	1,682,489	173,947
2001	28,093,759	1,507,062	179,359
2002	28,979,344	1,637,797	174,820
2003	24,664,137	1,611,407	154,346
2004	30,353,565	1,775,092	184,932
2005	32,430,856	1,833,721	204,138
2006	35,033,083	1,931,881	214,000
2007	36,701,556	1,918,159	221,000
2008	37,694,824	1,883,894	232,000
2009	37,203,978	1,633,791	240,360
2010	42,038,777	1,813,809	263,593
2011	46,500,000	1,870,000	301,700
2012	51,181,804	1,806,225	324,722
2013	53,726,087	1,850,233	343,800

Source: Singapore Changi Airport, 2015; Authors, 3030.

Hitherto the passenger traffic, airfreight and aircraft movements have been impressive but it cannot be taken for granted such a 'sweet' situation would continue to remain so. Singapore is not the only country investing in its airport infrastructure. Hong Kong's Chek Lap Kok Airport is among the Asian airports vying to defend its position as a major regional hub. Likewise, Bangkok and Kuala Lumpur are also upgrading their airports to become key transit points. A little further afield, there is also growing competition from Dubai in the Middle East, not least because of the aggressive growth of the region's airlines like Emirates, Etihad and Qatar Airways. Elsewhere, China is set to expand the total number of airports in the country to 230 in 2015 from 175 in 2010. Likewise, India has set a target of having 500 operational airports by 2020. Whilst this competitive trend would have repercussions on global travel patterns, which may well impact Changi Airport in the future, global travel may also open up new opportunities like the planning, development and management of airports and airport facilities, whereby the expertise capital from Singapore can potentially play some roles. This would be elaborated later in the discussion on the formation of the Changi Airport International. Therefore, the Changi Airport would have to continuously able to interrogate global air travel markets, innovate and respond, not only in terms of what to do but also when to do it. Hence, scenario planning becomes a useful and meaningful approach.

The Conceptual Framework

The scenario planning approach can be adopted to discuss the strategic planning of Changi Airport in Chapter 5, entailing a two-stage process. In the first stage, the conceptual framework is developed for the interrogation of the external environment so that it would provide the necessary building blocks, to ferment the development of a strategy map that deploys system dynamics. The conceptual framework integrates the competitive forces that Singapore's Changi Airport faces within the context of the potential strategic posture, which the Airport may choose and with the key business processes that support this strategic posture. In this way, every part of the ecosystem that supports the development and growth of Changi Airport would interface with key formation scenarios, thereby ensuring that the overall ecosystem is able to deal with the anticipated as well as the unexpected.

Fig 5.1 depicts the conceptual framework and highlights the relationships between the different components of the key scenarios as indicated by the 'spine' of Fig 4.1, the competitive strategy and the different business processes that deliver the strategy. Therefore, the scenarios are based on evolving trends in the following key factors:

a. Economic change at a national and global level.
b. Geo-political developments.

c. Ecology, environment and demography factors.
d. Aerospace technologies.
e. Evolving transport networks and travel patterns.
f. Developments in the global aerospace industry.

These key factors, individually and in combination, drive the scenarios that give rise to a range of threats and opportunities confronting the Changi Airport, its customers and suppliers. The threats and opportunities in turn would shape and influence the strategic positioning of Changi Airport and each of the business processes supporting the strategy.

Fig. 5.1. Conceptual Framework for Environmental Scanning

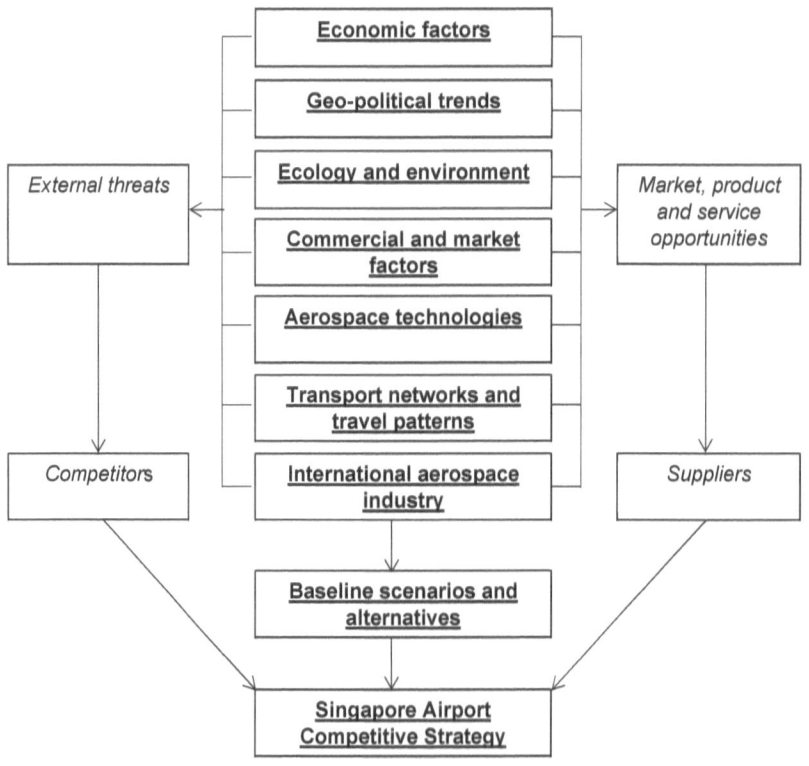

Source: Authors, 2020

System Dynamics Modelling

The strategic planning of Singapore's global Changi Airport can be analysed using the methodology of system thinking. Instead of the traditional linear and mechanistic way of thinking, system thinking adopts a non-linear and organic angle to establish the causal relationships between the various performance indicators (variables) in a dynamic or ever-changing manner (Sterman, 2002). One reason for the growing interest of non-linear systems has been the discovery of processes characterised by so called deterministic chaos i.e. processes generated by non-linear deterministic systems that evolve with high complexity (Aparicio et. al., 1999). The possibility that specific irregular oscillations of the economic variables can be explained by non-linear relations, rather than by exogenous shocks, shows itself to be of great importance, both for the interpretation of the nature of certain economic phenomenon, and for making forecasts like the way that the aviation industry, which is subject to multiple sources of uncertainties such as changes in technologies, political, social and economic factors. System dynamics modelling is both a continuum and an iteration of activities that range from conceptual to technical (Kwak, 1995). In practice, this continuum can be broadly structured into five main steps, involving problem definition, system conceptualisation, model formation and equation simulation, model validation and policy analysis. Specifically, the additional sophistication that can be handled with this methodology includes the following:

a. Ability to deal with feedback to form closed systems;
b. Allows for the interaction of variables in reinforcing and balancing loops that provide rich and realistic reflection of the real world;
c. Ability to handle delays. This is especially important and useful as investments in sports training would take some time to yield on-the-field results;

d. Predictive capabilities and simulations to facilitate scenario planning

The Aviation Performance Model

Based on the step-wise procedure discussed above, the primary factors initially discussed in the conceptual framework of Fig 5.1 are then morphed into an aviation performance model (APM) as depicted in Fig 5.2. The APM would highlight three independent variables, which can be regarded as the sub-industry sectors where specific strategies or actions can be taken to nurture and grow them. In other words, the well-being of these independent variables can be undertaken as the means to the eventual end, which is ultimately about what is good for the overall aviation industry of Singapore and of the Changi Airport in particular. These independent variables are identified as follows:

- The productive capacity of the Singapore economy (SE).
- Aviation and Aerospace Industry (AAI).
- Passenger and Cargo Services (PCS).

The well-being of the independent variables are leading indicators to how the operation-performance variables of the global Singapore Changi Airport can be indicated. These operational variables would be the dependent variables that are the lagging indicators. In the APM, these operation variables are identified as follows:

- Dependent variables:
- Aircraft Movement (AM).
- Passenger and cargo movement (PCM).

The magnitude of each of the independent and dependent variables would be regarded as the stocks in the systems modelling context, whereas the manner in which the stocks grow or decline would be regarded as flows.

Fig. 5.2. Framework for The System Dynamic Modelling of Changi Airport's Quest for Intrinsic Aircraft and Passenger Traffic

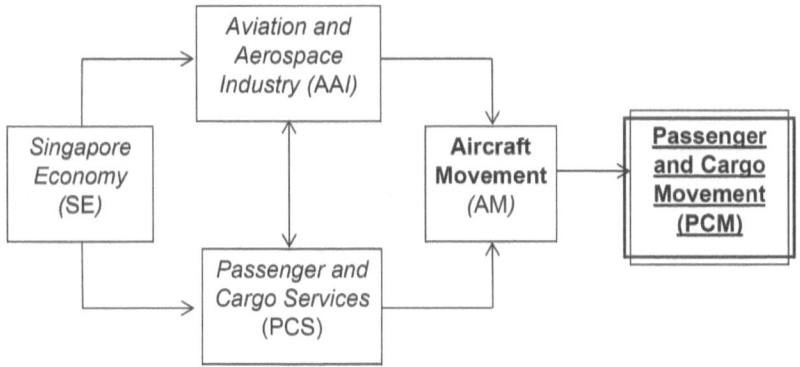

Source: Authors, 2020

In Fig 5.2, independent variables like the Singapore economy (SE), aviation and aerospace industry (AAI), and the passenger and cargo services (PCS) would interact and affect overall aircraft movement (AM), which is the intermediate dependent variable. However, AM is just the intermediate outcome that is desired. Ultimately, what the global Changi Airport wants is the quantum of PCM to grow. PCM is measured in terms of the number of passengers per year and number of tonnes of cargo handled per year. Fig 5.2 sets out the hypothesis that the strategic interests of stepping up PCM at Changi Airport need not be dependent on direct promotion of such passenger and cargo traffic to the Singapore global Changi Airport alone. While such rising PCM is still important and would still form the primary operational strategy, it must be acknowledged that the primary operational strategy can be easily replicated by any other airports. Indeed, owing to prevailing globalisation trend, which gives rise to the growing convergence of knowledge and the commoditization of products and services available at modern airports around the world. Therefore, the design and operational processes at modern airports around the world are gravitating towards something that are relatively similar. Travellers can attest to these relatively similar design and operational processes from their own personal experiences when travelling through various airports. The global Changi Airport would have to adopt additional strategies, which are unique to Singapore and are not easily replicated by others. Such additional strategies would invariably include the investment and expansion of other independent variables of the Singapore economy (SE) as a whole and the aviation and aerospace industry (AAI) in particular. However, any investments into SE and AAI would unlikely to be able to lead to immediate measurable outcomes. For e.g., the Seletar Aerospace Park, which is one of the key measures to expand the AAI would have taken a few years from conceptualisation to construction and to its eventual opening. Beyond that, the Seletar Aerospace Park would continue to evolve for many years to come.

Baseline Assessment with The Airport Performance Model (APM)

Aviation and The Aerospace Industry

Aircrafts need to carry out periodic maintenance, repair and overhaul services (MROS). Owing to the predominant availability of strong engineering skills, Singapore has become a much sought-after location by global airlines to obtain such MROS. As early as 2009, the aviation and aerospace industry in Singapore robustly contribute as much as a commendable S$14 billion in direct and indirect value-added to the Singapore GDP:

- S$8.7 billion of direct contribution from the MROS sector,
- S$3.1 billion through indirect contributions from the MROS sector's supply chain and
- S$2.4 billion from consumer spending by employees of the AAI sector and its supply chain.

Overall, 58,000 direct jobs were generated and available in the industry. The generated direct jobs would rise to 119,000 jobs if the entire supply chain is included. It is noteworthy from the efficiency perspective that the additional direct jobs generated is substantial and highly efficient at 61,000 direct jobs. Out of the available 58,000 direct jobs, the aerospace manufacturing companies employed approximately 18,000 people, the airline companies employed 15,000 people while the airports and ground service companies employed 24,000 people. The MROS sector also directly contributed S$1.5 billion in taxes rapidly enough by end 2009 (Aviation in Singapore, 2015), implying the sector's effectiveness to Singapore's economy. Another consideration is that the airlines registered in Singapore are major contributors to the economy. Collectively, they employ some 15,000 people in Singapore. The airlines provide a further 11,000 jobs in the supply chain by 2009. Such a fast pace of jobs and value-added contributions enable the airlines to substantially contribute over S$5.5 billion to the Singapore economy and 34,000 local jobs accordingly.

The high potential of the MROS have prompted the government to consider dedicating an industrial and business infrastructure in the form of an aerospace themed industrial estate to strengthen the growth of the aviation and aerospace industry (AAI). The options considered comprise the global Changi Airport complex or redeveloping the old Seletar Airport complex. The old Seletar Airport, which was originally built in 1928, has served as an airbase for the Royal Air Force (RAF) of Britain in the earlier days and for the Republic of Singapore Air Force (RSAF) more recently. Seletar Airport is also Singapore's primary facility for general aviation, which entails the use of private and smaller aircrafts. Its runway does not have sufficient length to handle the modern wide-body airliners. Nevertheless, the global Changi Airport may have the land to accommodate the complex aerospace park. The park's operations entail predominantly large wide-body airliners and may well be optimised if the traffic from the smaller and slower aircrafts can be diverted to the alternative airport like the old Seletar Airport. In the final analysis by the Economic Development Board and the Jurong Town Corporation (JTC Corp), the decision is taken to redevelop the old Seletar Airport to become the Seletar Aerospace Park (SAP). The SAP masterplan of about S$60 million worth of development occupies some 140 hectares of land, announced in Jun 2007. The SAP masterplan It comprises land for hosting aviation and aerospace related industries, and has direct access to the runway at the Seletar Airport. The runway is lengthened to handle the narrower body airliners like the Boeing 737 and the Airbus A320. Companies so engaged and, in the maintenance, repair and overhaul services (MROS) would find it synergistic to locate there. All these improvements and services would complement the other effort of developing the global Changi Airport to entrench the position of Singapore as the global aviation hub. Companies already located there include Singapore Technologies Aerospace, Jet Aviation, Eurocopter South East Asia and EADS Innovation Works

Rolls Royce PLC even has a facility there that concentrates on the assembly and testing of large civil engines like the Trent 1000 and Trent XWB, which are used in modern airliners like the Boeing 787 and the Airbus A350. However, owing to the relatively high cost structure in Singapore, there would be the pressure of demand for high end and 'high tech' services to be gradually shifted to other countries, with much lower costs structure. A balancing trend that is emerging is that the design and construction of aircrafts are becoming increasingly sophisticated with new and 'high tech' technologies like the greater use of composites to reduce weight and the use of more advanced engines. Such developments may well offer Singapore a niche to continue to be viable and competitive for MROS for state-of-the-art aircrafts. Commemorative events the launching of the Seletar Airport with its new runway as part of the Seletar Aerospace Hub in 2007; the opening of Seletar Aerospace Park by Mr LIM Hng Kiang, the former and talented Minister for Trade and Industry; the official visit by the Duke and Duchess of Cambridge, Prince William and his wife Catherine to the aero-engine maker Rolls-Royce and its massive S$700 million engine and fan blade facility at Seletar

Aerospace Park on 12 September 2012, where they unveiled the first Rolls-Royce aero engine assembled and tested in Singapore - the Trent 900 that powers the Airbus 380. The new engine is the first of 20 that the British engine-maker would roll out in 2012 at. Seletar. Production would be ramped up to 250 engines and 6,000 fan blades by 2016. The facility would also produce the Trent1000 engines, which would be used in the B787 Dreamliner.

Beyond the MRO sector, the Seletar Aerospace Park would support corporate and general aviation. It is already the home base for several smaller charter aircraft operations serving regional corporate travel, aeromedical evacuations as well as charter brokers. There are also aviation consulting companies specialising in regional aircraft ownership and operation like the Asian Corporate Aviation Management and Asia Corporate Jet. Another important goal is to complete a comprehensive offering that Singapore can offer as a global aviation hub is the Singapore Air Show. This event, which was formerly known as the Changi Global Air Show, is a biennial aerospace event held in Singapore starting from 2008. The event is launched as a strategic partnership between Singaporean agencies, the Civil Aviation Authority of Singapore (CAAS(and the Defence Science and Technology Agency (DSTA) after the relocation of Asian Aerospace to Singapore. The significance of staging such an event is not just for the organizers to earn rental income from the exhibitors.

More important, with the event attracting the major suppliers and purchasers as well as thought leaders in the industry, the event helps to cement Singapore's position as a global, reputable and great place to conduct business and forge collaborations in the aviation industry. The Singapore Air Show Aviation Leadership Summit, which is the only event of its kind in the industry that brings together high-level participants from regulators, private sector, governments and airline operators, to address a wide range of topics from environment, liberalisation and security challenges to salient strategic trends the region faces. Leveraging on such activities as the foundation, other policy or research conferences may also be held to continually improve the regulatory environment for open skies (Baker, 2014).

Fig. 5.3. Development Thrust for the Aviation and Aerospace Industry

Source: Authots, 2020

Passenger and Cargo Services (PCS)

Singapore's global Changi Airport has quickly evolved to become an aviation due primarily to its strategic location. In the early days, inter-continental flights between Europe and Australia are subject to a maximum distance, an aircraft can fly without refuelling, Singapore had become a natural stopover point and to some extent the rest of South East and East Asian regions. With advances in aircraft technology for the Boeing 777X and Airbus A350, which can fly non-stop to almost anywhere in the world, some air routes that did previously depend on a Singapore stopover would no longer be needed. Therefore, the direct routes between the cities of origin and the destination would occur without passing through Singapore, posing a threat to Singapore. While Singapore can continue to leverage on its hub advantage, it should no longer rely on such an advantage alone to compete. Singapore has to ensure that its offering of routine and heavy maintenance, repair and overhaul services (MROS).are of the highest standard and quality for the airlines' aircrafts. Singapore must ensure that its passenger and cargo services are world class. Singapore should soft and hard sell to passengers, wanting to visit and come to Singapore, to savour the unique and memorable Singapore experience that comprise the following:

- multi-cultural food variety,
- multi-racial and multi-religious harmony,
- hawker meals centres,
- gourmet dining restaurants,
- local outdoor sports and recreation,
- casino and entertainment centres,
- world class road and rail transport, music, theatre and the arts
- International 4- ad 5- star hotel and serviced apartments.

In effect, the passengers are just not meant for transit.

Therefore, the quality of services and the availability of adequate capacity to serve passengers and cargo at Singapore's global Changi Airport are critical to attract airlines to use Singapore as their hub. There are three terminals at the Changi Airport as at 2015. These are Terminals 1, 2 and 3 or simply T1, T2, and T3. When T1 first opened in 1981, it had a capacity of only 11 million passengers a year. T1's capacity is subsequently more than doubled with the lengthening of the finger piers and other operational improvements. The three operational terminals in Changi Airport collectively have a total handling capacity of 66 million passengers annually. T1, T2 and T3 are directly connected with one another via a people mover system. This people mover system is available at the landside or the public area and the airside within the transit area that is restricted to passengers. Since the opening of T1 in 1981, T2 in 1990, and T3 in 2008, Singapore's global Changi Airport has been voted regularly as the world's best airport. The recent awards received is shown in Table 5.2.

Table 5.2. The Top Ten Airports in the World

Rank	Airport Name
1	Singapore Changi Airport

2	Incheon International Airport
3	Munich Airport
4	Hong Kong International Airport
5	Amsterdam Schiphol Airport
6	Tokyo International Airport Haneda
7	Beijing Capital International Airport
8	Zurich Airport
9	Vancouver International Airport
10	London Heathrow Airport

Source: Authors, 2020; www.worldairportwards.com, 2015

In addition, there is the Budget Terminal conceived and built in 2006. The year is the nascent period in the evolution of budget air travel. To keep costs low, airports like Singapore's global Changi Airport and the Kuala Lumpur International Airport (KLIA) provide separate terminals with scaled down amenities like aerobridges. The design and construction of such facilities is devoid of elaborate physical structures and decorations. Changi's budget terminal is originally designed to handle a relatively modest scale of 2.7 million passengers a year. This budget terminal is subsequently expanded to reach 7 million passengers annually. However, this terminal has been closed since 2012 to make way for the construction of Terminal 4 (T4), which is scheduled to complete in 2017 and with an impressive annual capacity of 16 million passengers. Instead on just relying on inexpensive design and construction to save on costs, T4 is designed to enable efficient passenger processing and the quick turnaround of aircraft without compromising the travellers' experience. Specifically, T4 is designed to cater primarily to narrow body aircrafts like the Boeing 737 and the Airbus A320, which is the main aircraft type for flights within Asia. With T4 coming on stream, The Singapore global Changi Airport's annual capacity would reach 82 million by 2017 that would provide a headroom for more than 50% traffic growth, from its traffic volume of 53 million passenger movements (AFP, 2013). This added capacity would allow Singapore's global Changi Airport to cater to the anticipated 5% annual capacity growth, in conjunction with the ASEAN Open Skies agreement,

2015. Transport Minister LUI Tuck Yew (second from left) had been the guest of honour to commemorate the launch and model the new Changi Airport Terminal 4, ready by 2017. His entourage did include Mr Lee Seow Hiang, CEO of Changi Airport Group (CAG); Mr Liew Mun Leong, Chairman of CAG and Mr David Buffonge, company Director of Benoy Limited.

Nevertheless, an airport's terminal buildings are primarily transport infrastructure. As a function, the terminal buildings serve their purpose adequately. Athanassopoulos (2013) alludes to the conceptual thinking that airport complexes for the 21st century need to go beyond mere transport infrastructure. In particular, Singapore's global Changi Airport has leveraged on its sterling rack record for creating a unique and lasting experience for travellers, and to position itself as a signature lifestyle destination for travellers and the local population. The latest development that would propel the global Changi Airport's growth in such a new signature lifestyle destination is the S$1.47 billion 'Jewel' project, announced in 2013. Mixed use Jewel project would house top class amenities, dining and retail space that would serve terminals T1, T2 and T3. The Jewel project even provides passenger facilities for check-in, the training of airport staff and an international grade hotel (Sim, 2013). Beyond amenities, the scale and grandeur of the Jewel project would make it a global destination for travellers and the local population.

Beyond T4, a fifth terminal, Terminal 5 (T5), which incorporates a third runway has been conceptualised and announced in 2013. T5 would be built on 1,080 hectares of reclaimed land east of the existing runway 2 of the Singapore global Changi Airport. Unlike T2, T3 and T4 which can be considered as part and parcel of the organic addition to annual passenger capacities, T5 would have the annual capacity in excess of 50 million passengers p.a. that is almost as many as that of T1 to T3 combined. Upon completion, T5 would become one of the largest airport terminals in the world. With the additional capacity from T5 when it is completed in the mid-2020s, Singapore's global Changi Airport eventually has the overall capacity in excess of 130 million passengers p.a., making it amongst the largest airport in the world alongside the Atlanta, Beijing and London airports. It is noteworthy that Mrs Josephine TEO, then Minister of State for Finance and Transport, did launch the book on the Singapore global Changi Airport's history with Mdm WAN Fook Yin, widow of Mr HOWE Yoon Chong, the individual who had come up with Changi as the site for Singapore's first global Changi Airport. The late Mr HOWE was Chairman of the special committee on airport development in 1975. He passed on in 2007, aged 84. Madam WAN is handed the book in a ceremony on 18 July 2012, to mark the completion of renovation works of Terminal 1.

While T5 would bring about a massive capacity increase in the Singapore global Changi Airport, its significance would go beyond that. It would in fact usher in a new era, as it has happened previously when the airport of Singapore evolved from Kallang to Paya Lebar, to Singapore's global Changi Airport T1 to 4 and the Jewel project, and eventually to Changi T5.

Table 5.3. The Busiest Airports in the World

Rank	Airport	Passengers 2014
1.	Atlanta International Airport, USA.	96,178,899
2.	Beijing Capital International Airport, China.	86,130,390
3.	London Heathrow Airport, UK.	73,408,442
4.	Tokyo Haneda Airport, Japan.	72,826,862
5.	Los Angeles Airport, USA.	70,665,472
6.	Dubai Airport, Dubai.	70,475,636
7.	O'Hare Airport, USA.	70,015,746
8.	Paris-Charles de Gaulle Airport, France.	63,808,796
9.	Dallas/Fort Worth Airport, USA.	63,523,489
10.	Hong Kong Airport, Hon g Kong.	63,148,379
11.	Frankfurt Airport, Germany.	59,566,132
12.	Soekarno-Hatta Airport, Indonesia.	57,005,406
13.	Istanbul Atatürk Airport, Turkey.	56,767,108
14.	Amsterdam Airport Schiphol, Netherland.	54,978,023
15.	Guangzhou Baiyun Airport, China.	54,780,346
16.	Singapore Changi Airport, Singapore.	54,091,802

Source: Authors, 2929; Airports Council International (http://www.aci.aero/), 2015

Fig. 5.4. Evolution of the Airports In Singapore

Source: Authors, 2020

While passenger services are more visible to the general public, the Singapore global Changi Airport serves an additional segment that is less visible. Nonetheless, it is an equally important part of aviation - the airfreight or cargo segment. In the case of Singapore, such a segment is not only important from the perspective of the logistics and transhipment business *per se*, but it is also crucial to the manufacturing, trading, and import of critical commodities like food and other perishables for domestic consumption. For the MRO business that is discussed earlier, the airfreight and cargo segment would just contribute to additional demand and business opportunities.

The infrastructure for cargo services at the Singapore global Changi Airport is provided in the forms of the Changi Airfreight Centre (CAC), the Airport Logistics Park Singapore (ALPS), and the Coolport. This infrastructure is within the Free Trade Zone (FTZ), where transhipment cargo can be broken down and reconsolidated with minimal Customs formalities. Specifically, the Coolport incorporates multi-tiered zones with varying temperatures from -28 degree C to 18 degree C to cater to the handling of perishables likes pharmaceuticals, food, flowers and other commodities that need to be maintained within the cold logistics chain.

Like the passenger terminals, the availability of comprehensive business solutions for airfreight has attracted airlines across the world, couriers and third-party logistics companies to set up their regional operations hubs in Singapore. The FTZ is appropriately located in the airport compound, together with logistics centres in the vicinity of the Singapore's complementary global Changi Airport. Included close by is the Loyang and Changi South industry estate. Singapore's chronic land scarcity and the high cost of land always poses a constraint to Singapore in its quest to develop businesses that require direct real estate, in particular land for warehousing and distribution parks. The distinguishing factor that Singapore can lean on to sustain its competitive edge would be to leverage on its strength, to offer reliable and timely services for cargo of high value or high security.

The Industrial Capacity of the Singapore Economy (SE)

Beyond the aviation and aerospace industry, the industrial capacity of the Singapore economy is also an integral part of the Singapore global Changi Airport's strategic design. As more services and industries are set up in Singapore to serve the rest of the world, it is expected that the number of travellers and cargo going through the airport is bound to rise strongly. The Singapore economy is likened to be a highly developed trade-oriented market economy. Some of the accolades that best articulate what they mean include being ranked as the most open economy in the world, the least corrupt, the most pro-business and with low tax rates, and the third highest per-capita GDP worldwide in purchasing power parity (PPP). Singapore has benefited from the inward flow of foreign direct investments (FDI) from global investors and institutions, owing to her highly attractive investment climate and stable political environment.

Singapore's key manufacturing activities include the chemicals, petrochemicals, oil refining, ship-building and repair, wafer fabrication, and the pharmaceuticals sectors. Singapore's service sectors are very competent and effective and they include finance, tourism, legal, engineering, computing, research, technology and education. To preserve and further promote its global standing and foot print, Singapore is pursuing other measures to promote innovation, creativity, to encourage entrepreneurship, to re-train or upskill her workforce, to maintain an open-door approach to attract talented people worldwide. All such measures contribute to the sustainable and modest growth of the economy. Various courses and joint studies specific and relevant to the aerospace and aviation sector are readily available at the universities and polytechnics. The Institute of Technical Education (ITE) trains people in aerospace engineering and aviation management. In addition, the Building and Control Authority (BCA) Academy, the Singapore Aviation Academy (SAA) of the Civil Aviation Authority of Singapore (CAAS) offers a wide range of operational, management and technocentric programmes, which are benchmarked to international standards and best practices, to meet the training needs of the global aviation community.

The above-mentioned courses and joint studies would converge not only to boost Singapore's productivity, natural and competitive advantages but also the knowledge capital of the country. Collectively, Singapore remains pro- business, pro-competitive and ready for the challenges of an information-, technology-, research and development driven global economy. In the context of the Singapore global Changi Airport, all the industries and sectors of the Singapore economy at large should inevitably generate the sustainable, fast and reliable movement of travellers and goods though the Airport. The industries and sectors would provide the critical mass that makes it attractive for airliners to direct their air routes through Singapore, and on which the airliners can fully develop their passenger transit and cargo transhipment business in the steady state. Rising robust wealth and powers of the Asian countries like China, India and Indonesia provide the impetus to step up viable demand for travel in the mid and long term. Thereafter, the accession of the ASEAN Economic Community and the Trans Pacific Partnership Agreement

(TPPA) may well be additional future changes that potentially boost and support growth of the aviation and aerospace sector.

The Way Forward for Singapore SG50

it is interesting and noteworthy that what started off as mere facilities and physical infrastructural provision with limited scale to support the needs of the Singapore, has evolved to become a global transhipment centre. Undeniably, the achievements in terms of the developments of Singapore's global Changi Airport and global seaport hub are more or less achieved beyond expectation. But what about the future? Can the approach that has brought much success over the past 50 years be still applicable in the next 50 years? To answer such questions, one has to examine the macro environment existing then, now and those projected for the future. 50 years ago, in say the 1960s, Singapore is one of the few relatively modern cities in the Asia region. Unlike Singapore's larger neighbours that have to contend with the challenges to resolve the different kinds of development needs and painfully structural adjustment, from having a larger rural hinterland, Singapore as a city island state could largely focus its economic development and learning curve via connecting itself directly with the rest of the world.

Fast forward to the present day, Singapore no longer enjoys such a direct benefit or at least that the benefit is no longer as distinct as it was before. The rest of the world including Singapore's neighbouring countries have made progress by leaps and bounds. For instance, Bangkok and Kuala Lumpur have developed modern mega airports that are comparable to Singapore's global Changi Airport in terms of scale and architectural designs. On the basis of 63.3 million passengers handled as recent as 2014, a much larger annual passenger capacity than Singapore's global Changi's annual passenger capacity of 54 million passengers, the Hong Kong Chek Lap Kok Airport has already rolled out its Masterplan 2030, which would bring its capacity to 97 million passengers per year. In comparison, the Dubai

International Airport handles some 70 million passengers. Dubai's second airport, the Al Maktoum International Airport has also commenced operations. Such a second airport is planned to eventuate the capacity of 160 to 260 million passengers annually. In terms of seaports, the throughput of Shanghai has already surpassed that of Singapore's since 2010. Compounding the challenge from intense competition, most of these other cities do not face the one constraint that Singapore has but would not be able overcome, namely the limited availability of land for continual expansion of its physical infrastructural facilities. In the case of the global airport, there is also a similar constraint concerning the potential overcrowding of airspace for the queuing of aircrafts, arriving at and leaving from Singapore.

Beyond the challenge of scale, there are also macro issues to deal with. For instance, aircrafts may choose to travel direct to the destinations without going through Singapore for transhipment or transit. There would be a need for more sophisticated information management systems to sort the myriad of cargoes of various forms, and to deliver the cargoes to customers within an ever increasingly demanding time line. The aviation and aerospace sector faces a key challenge that one of the more popular air routes is the 'Kangaroo' route between London and Sydney. Many airlines ply such a route including a stopover in Singapore. With the development of longer-range aircraft like the Boeing 777 and the Airbus A350, direct flights between London and Sydney may become technologically feasible and commercially viable. The emergence of mega aircrafts like the Airbus 380, which can carry more than 600 passengers, would mitigate this direct flight threat to some extent. The economic justifications for the such mega aircrafts are founded on the hub and spoke transportation framework. Therefore, Singapore's global Changi Airport has been working collaboratively with airlines, aircraft manufacturers and like-minded global stakeholders to enhance developments that support greater value add to customers via the hub and spoke transportation framework. Indeed, the Singapore Airlines (SIA) actively launch customers for the A380. Such an action by SIA can be deemed to be an integrated approach to enable Singapore Inc secure and advance overall aviation interest for Singapore.

It is essential that Singapore would have to turn its smallness to an advantage. The constraint of size has spurred innovations in design and optimisation. The proposed development of Terminal 5 (T5) at Singapore's global Changi Airport and the Seletar Aviation Park should spawn further growth in aviation traffic and related engineering services. The shift of the airport from Paya Lebar to Changi in 1980 and start to completion of Changi T5's construction, should well offer favourable innovations to help negate some of Singapore's constraints, to renew and extend Singapore's competitive edge. However, favourable physical infrastructure alone is not sufficient to sustain the competitive edge. To borrow an analogy from the sports discipline, physical infrastructure offers at best 'what it takes to play', which may not be sufficient to ensure victory. To sustain Singapore's competitive edge in the intense competition to be global air gateways, physical infrastructure developments undertaken by Singapore would have to include innovations in terms of design and the, deployment of the state-of-the-art technologies that set leading standards and the benchmark for land and labour productivities, the bundling of services for seamless integration, and effective management being actively responsive to address customer needs. Significant developments in parallel_have taken place in the Singapore aviation and aerospace sector. The regulatory functions have been consolidated at the Civil Aviation Authority of Singapore (CAAS). CAAS takes the lead in Singapore for policy coordination and negotiation with other relevant global regulatory bodies like the Global Civil Aviation Organization (ICAO). Business functions have been spawned into corporatized global gateway owners and operators like the Changi Airport Group (CAG). It is hoped that public and private sector flexibility and commercial discipline readily offer the impetus to grow public and private sector organisations to greater heights of achievement.

Indeed, the development journey of Singapore's airports has evolved to be an essential part of the intellectual property of Singapore vested with Singapore's global Changi Airport. The latter would form partnership with companies and organisations in Singapore and overseas to venture into the business of designing, building, investing and managing seaports in various parts of the world. As Singapore develops, matures and becomes a thought leader in infrastructure development and operations, there are now 'replicas' of Singapore in the form of airports designed, developed and/or operated by Singapore institutions notably in:

Brazil	Turkey,	Korea
Russia,	Panama,	Japan
Belgium,	Argentina,	India
Italy,	Columbia	Saudi Arabia
Portugal,	China,	Thailand,
Vietnam	Indonesia.	

More than competition on size alone, Singapore would have to approach it from the total package of the provision of good and reliable business solutions, which would add value to customers.

Institutionalising Research &Development (R & D)t

While money can buy physical infrastructure developments but once built, physical infrastructure developments are likely to remain and last for some years to come. However, there are other considerations in the whole gamut of sustaining a repertoire of globally competitive seaports like trade patterns, technologies, consumer behaviour that continuously evolve and change over time. Business models and/or operational strategies may even become obsolete and need to be refreshed or reinvented from time to time. Assumptions need to be revisited and reviewed. Innovations need to be tested and validated. Accordingly, the successes hitherto can only sustain if Singapore invests continuously in research and development (R & D), which in turn require investments in its people. Such people investments would entail nurturing engineers, lawyers, planners, managers add economists, who are rooted in the contextual domains of transportation, logistics and physical infrastructure.

In addition, such people investments should embrace outstanding work ethics, a global mind set and the ability to operate and collaborate in a multi-disciplinary and multi-cultural environment. The introduction of highly relevant people-investment courses in the local polytechnics and universities would be a step in the desired direction. Beyond that, the setting up of research centres and think-tanks, hosting of global conferences, seminars and the provision of research funding, all of which act collectively to facilitate the growth of a conducive ecosystem for sustainable development. A Key example is the Singapore Aviation Academy (SAA)to advance learning, training, library information and data sourcing, communication and interaction among airport manpower, specialist courses at the graduate certificate, diploma and master levels. In the final analysis, it is hoped that the reflections and discussions in Chapter 5 would contribute towards further enriching the Singapore conversation to turn the constraints it faces into opportunities. So far, the combination of rationale thinking, hard work, a favourable geo-political location and good fortune have endured fortuitously to formulate the air gateway, to Singapore's benefit.

While it may not have been purposefully coordinated as such at the onset, it is interesting to note that similar approaches have taken place in Singapore's airport developments over time. In the aviation and aerospace sector, the Singapore global Changi Airport and the Changi Airport Group (CAG) continue to play the central role of keeping both entities 'ship shape' and viable, of running efficiently, effectively and innovatively, and of actively engaging in and regularly reviewing strategic and corporate planning. The Seletar Aerospace Park, developed by JTC Corp, continue to attract, establish and advance new and high technology tenants and lessees of the aviation and aerospace sector. Indeed, it is hoped that Chapter 5 has heightened the awareness and realisation of the importance of policy development from the whole of government perspective, and thereby promote even greater inter-agency cooperation and collaborations.

As Singapore sails into its next 50 years of nation building, it would face the challenges of a more complex and more competitive world. Singapore should stay the course to strive to have pro-business and wealth distributive policies, talented professionals and those with the 'nose' for business and high enough risk-adjusted return enterprise. There is the urgency for superior in-house project execution and management our airports to the next level of success (Figure 5.1). Singapore has the greater responsibility as a developed country to contribute to the betterment of the world. Therefore, Singapore has started to leverage on its experience to help countries develop and operate their fledgling airports. Singapore has stepped up efforts in training, R & D with various programmes implemented at its institutions of higher learning, think thanks and research funding. The next 50 years should hold out the promise to be not only exciting but also more wholesome. The next 50 years should be an era when a 'grown up' Singapore would be an active contributor, towards enhancing the body of knowledge in physical infrastructure provision and management, to the betterment of the world.

It would be a major omission if Chapter 5 does not acknowledge the many generations of workers, who have contributed to make viable and sustainable Singapore's airports of today. Singapore should also count itself fortunate to have many strategic partners and friends in the form of businesses and companies, who believe in the Singapore story and who made Singapore part of their global strategies by locating their businesses here, or leveraging on Singapore as a strategic pivot to conduct their businesses and operations in the Asia Pacific region. Let us hope that such strategic partnerships and alliances would continue to thrive in the next 50 years and beyond.

Fig. 5.1. Reinforcing Causal Loops Set Within A System Dynamic Model for Sustainable Developments of Gateways, Singapore

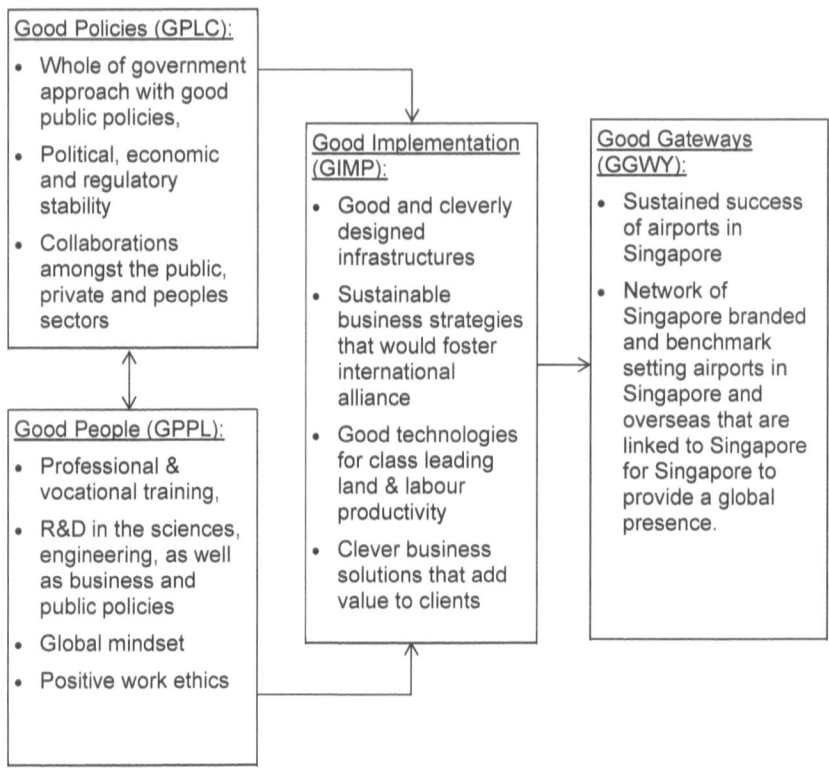

Source: Authors, 2020

Concluding Remarks

In financial instruments investing like that of common stocks, bonds, direct and indirect real estate, both thetechnical and fundamental analyses are often conducted to offer a reference for decision makers. Likewise, and in public physical infrastructure developments like the Singapore global Changi Airport, public funding is also a form of investment that entails uncertainties, which need to be rigorously evaluated with financial modelling on the risks and returns. Beyond financial returns, public physical infrastructural investing like Singapore's global Changi Airport seek to pursue a larger strategic objective for the long-term, well-being of the nation. In this regard, the Changi Airport is not just a public infrastructure, but also a key pillar of strength to support the growth of Singapore's trade-oriented market economy. Specifically, Singapore serves as the home base for another national institution like the ubiquitous Singapore Airlines (SIA), itself a market leader in the airline business.

Indeed, beyond airport development *per se*, the provision for the expansion of Singapore's global Changi Airport with its third and fourth runways, would eventuate significant contribution to Singapore's urban renewal and development. While the third runway would primarily be for civil aviation in conjunction with the development of terminal T5, the fourth runway would be for the eventual relocation of the RSAF Paya Lebar Air Base to the Changi East district. When the T5 and fourth runway developments materialise, this would free up some 800 ha of land, currently occupied by the RSAF Paya Lebar Air Base, is meant for housing, industry, recreation and other uses. The additional freed up land of 800 ha of land would enable Singapore's Urban Redevelopment Authority (URA) to liberalise the height restrictions around the Paya Lebar district, currently necessary to facilitate military air operations. Consequently, a lot of more urban redevelopment projects can be so planned and undertaken, to safeguard an even cleaner, greener, much less noisy, mixed-use built environment for Singaporeans; and to create more space for industrial and economic developments. Corresponding to these developments, the organisations that plan and execute the developments over the years have also evolved.

Prior to 2009, the Civil Aviation Authority of Singapore (CAAS) is the body in charge of developments and operations of airports in Singapore. Thereafter, the business aspects of the CAAS is corporatized to form the Changi Airport Group (CAG). Beyond managing the Changi Airport *per se*, CAG also invests in and manages foreign airports through its subsidiary Changi Airports International (CAI). CAI's goal is to build a quality portfolio of airport investments worldwide with strong markets and significant development potential.

Key CAI business activities include investments in airports, the provision of consultancy and airport management services. Today, CAI's presence covers major economies like that for China, India, the Middle East and Europe. It is imperative that the investment appraisal and assessment of the Singapore global Changi Airport has to be based on a combination of financial analysis with strategic and business considerations. Chapter 5 has demonstrated how the development of the airport performance model (APM) on the basis of economic conceptions and the principles of system modelling can be readily adopted to support scenario planning and policy analysis. The airport performance model (APM) and Chapter 5 would be beneficial to policy makers and investors by providing them with a structured framework to consider the questions they are seeking to answer, and the decisions that they would need to make. It is acknowledged that the APM can potentially be expanded to include more factors, and to deal with more complexities. It is hoped that the work in this Chapter offers a preliminary platform to stimulate research endeavours in public policy analysis, especially in projecting future performance of physical transport infrastructural provision, within the context of portfolio management and its resource constrained optimisation. Beyond that, actual economic data can also be inputted into such models for scenarios generation to support policy development and decision making. Such big data analysis and scenario planning should open up a wide field for policy research, by way of reinforcing loop(s) to contribute towards making Singapore a knowledge and research centre for the aviation and aerospace sector.

References

Airports Council International. http://www.aci.aero/

Aparicio, T, Pozo, E., Saura, D. 1999. Investigating chaotic behavior in economic series: the delay time in the grassberger procaccia algorithm. GlobalJournal of Theoretical & Applied Finance, vol. 2, p. 357.

Athanassopoulos, A. 2013. Airport design history and evolution: Towards an environmental approach. Journal of Transportation Law, Logistics and Policy. Second Quarter 2013, Vol 8 Issue 2, p118-129.

Aviation in Singapore. http://en.wikipedia.org/wiki/Aviation_in_Singapore.

Baker, C. Asian Aviation Magazine. March 2014, Vol. 12 Issue 2, p23-23.

Brevetti, F. Hutchison hungry for privatisation deals. Seatrade Review. September 1996.

Changi Airport Group Annual Report, various issues.

Clark, R C., Pledger, M., Needler, H M J. Risk analysis in the evaluation of non-aerospace projects. Project Management. Vol. 8 No. 1. February 1990.

Burnson, Patrick. Surveys Find Global 3PLs Experiencing Significant Success Across the Supply Chain Industry. SCMR, 28 September, 2015. http://www.logisticsmgmt.com.

Button, Kenneth. Transport economics. Edward Elgar Publishing, 2010.

Chapman, C., Cooper, D. Risk Analysis for Large Projects, Models, Methods, and Cases. John Wiley & Sons. 1987.

Checkland, P., Scholes, J. Soft Systems Methodology in Action. John Wiley & Sons. 1990.

Cheng, Leonard K., Wong, Yue-Chim Richard. Port Facilities and Container Handling Services: The Hong Kong Economic Policy Studies. City University of Hong Kong Press, Hong Kong. 1997.

Civil Aviation Authority of Singapore Annual Reports, various issues.

Cullinane, K., Wang T F., Cullinane, S. Container Terminal Development in Mainland China and Its Impact on the Competitiveness of the Port of Hong Kong. Transport Reviews. Volume 24, Issue 1, 2004. pages 33-56.

Developing Singapore into a global integrated logistics hub. The Economic Review Committee Working Group on Logistics. 2012

Funtowicz, Silvio O., Ravetz, Jerome R. "Uncertainty and Quality in Science for Policy." Kluwer Academic Publishers. 1990.

J R M., Lee, P M., Lucas, H C. A resource-based view of competitive advantage at the Port of Singapore. The Journal of Strategic Information Systems. Volume 14, Issue 1, March 2005, Pages 69–86

Hargitay, Stephen E., YU, Shi-Ming. Property Investment Decisions - A Quantitative Approach. E & FN SPON. 1993.

Ho, K H D. An Econometric Model Simulating the Effects of Seaport Policy and National Economic Development in Singapore. Journal of Real Estate and Construction, 1994. 4: 29 - 47.

H. Arjen van Klink., Geerke C. van den Berg. Gateways and intermodalism. Journal of Transport Geography. Vol. 6, No. 1. 1998. 1-9.

Headland, J.; E, W.; Thompson, L.; Breeman, P. Balancing Port Planning: Demand, Capacity, Land, Cost, Environment and Uncertainty. Ports 2004. ASCE Conference Proceedings.

Ho, K H D. The Seaport Economy. Singapore University Press. 1996.

Ho, K H D., Ho, M.W., Hui, E. Structural Dynamics in the Policy Planning of Large Infrastructure Investment Under the Competitive Environment". Journal of Urban Planning and Development, American Society of Civil Engineers. 2007.

Ho, M. W., Ho, K H D. Risk Management in Large Physical Infrastructure Investment. The Journal of the Maritime Economics and Logistics. (2006)

Hong Kong Annual Digest of Statistics. Various issues. Census and Statistics Department, Hong Kong.

Hong Kong Port Cargo Forecasts. Various Issues. Hong Kong Port and Maritime Board.

HUGHES, D. Singapore and HK both face competition for hub port status. Business Times. 22 Jul 1996.

Hui, Eddie C. M., Seabroke, Wouldiam., Wong, Gordon K. C. (2004).Forecasting Cargo Throughput for the Port of Hong Kong: Error Correction Model Approach. Journal of Urban Planning and Development. ASCE. Vol: 130(4). December, 2004.

Jones, Clive Vaugham. "Financial risk analysis of infrastructure deb: the case of water and power investments". Quorum Books. 1991.

Kaur, K. Seletar hub expected to run out of space in a decade, next phase of sector's development being planned. http://www.straitstimes.com/singapore/. 10 Feb. 2016.

Kia M.; Shayan E.; Ghotb, F. Investigation of port capacity under a new approach by computer simulation. Computers and Industrial Engineering, Vol 42, No. 11. April 2002, pp. 533-540(8). Elsevier Science.

Konings, J. W. Integrated centres for the transhipment, storage, collection and distribution of goods: A survey of the possibilities for a high-quality intermodal transport concept. Transport Policy. Vol 3, No. 1, 1996. 3-11.

Kwak, S. 1995, Policy analysis of Hanford tank farm operations with system dynamic approach, Department of Nuclear Engineering, Massachusetts Institute of Technology, Cambridge, MA.

Lee, H. L. Singapore: Long-term vision is to become a global city. Global. http://www.global-briefing.org.

Lee, S H. 2001. Container Port Begins to Show Crisis: A Solution Should be Devised Early. Hong Kong Economic Journal, 6 December 2001.

Lohmann, G., Albers, S., Koch, B., Pavlovich, K. From hub to tourist destination – An explorative study of Singapore and Dubai's aviation-based transformation. Journal of Air Transport Management. Volume 15, Issue 5, September 2009, Pages 205–211

Long-Term Market. http://www.boeing.com.

Maritime and Port Authority Annual Reports, various issues.

Mustafa, Muhammad A., Al-Bahar, Jamal, F. Project Risk Assessment Using the Analytic Hierarchy Process. In IEEE Transactions on Engineering management. Vol. 38. No. 1. February 1991.

Ngai, L C., Lin, K Pui K. The Development of Port Facilities in Hong Kong and Southern China. 6th Asia Pacific Sea Transport Conference, 1997.

Panayides, P M. Maritime logistics and global supply chains: towards a research agenda. Maritime Economics & Logistics. Vol 8, no. 1. 2006. 3-18.

Phang S Y. Strategic development of airport and rail infrastructure: the case of Singapore. Transport Policy. Volume 10, Issue 1, January 2003, Pages 27–33

Rodrigue, J.P. The largest available container ship, 1975-2015. https://people.hofstra.edu/geotrans/

Seah, P. Changi Airport: A significant story for Singapore's young. http://www.ipscommons.sg/. 17 Mar 2015.

Seletar Aerospace Park. http://jtc.gov.sg.

Sim, R. Project Jewel at Changi Airport to cost $1.47b. The Straits Times. 23 December 2013. http://news.asiaone.com/news.

Singapore Changi Airport, 2015. http://en.wikipedia.org/wiki/Singapore_Changi_Airport.

Singapore to double capacity of Changi Airport. https://sg.news.yahoo.com.

Sterman, J.. Business dynamics: System thinking and modeling for a complex world. McGraw-Hill. New York. 2000

TAN, C M. 42 years, 500 million TEU containers, one PSA. http://www.straitstimes.com/opinion/. Jun 22, 2015.

The world's Best Airports are announced at the World Airport Awards. http://www.worldairportawards.com.

TPP deal: US and 11 other countries reach landmark Pacific trade pact. http://www.theguardian.com/business/2015/oct/05/

Wang, C. Ducruet, C. New port development and global city making: emergence of the Shanghai–Yangshan multilayered gateway hub. Journal of Transport Geography. Volume 25, November 2012, Pages 58–69

Wang, J J. The Formation of Hong Kong-Shenzhen Container Load Center. Researches on Shipping Market and Management" Proceeding of GlobalConference on Shipping and Shipping Market Facing 21 Century, 1998.

Yong, Mei Fong. "Asian Ports may face demand of 104m boxes in 2000". Business Times, 4 October 1996.

Youngson, A.J. "Overhead capital: a study in development economics." Edinburgh University Press. 1967.

CHAPTER 6

THE CONCLUSION & REFERENCES

Chapter 10 summarises the book's findings and highlights the contributions and recommendations made. Chapter 1 examines the relationship between seaport throughput and seaport capacity expansion. Discussions leveraged on case studies of the Seaports of Singapore and Hong Kong as they share similarities but that they have chosen different strategic growth paths, appropriate for the geo-political and economic circumstances each of them faces. Given the political and economic integration between Hong Kong and mainland China, Hong Kong has devolved some of its previous seaport roles to the newer China seaports, particularly those seaports in the Pearl River Delta. While Singapore has continued to invest in and deploy newer and larger terminals equipped with the state-of-the-art technology, to further develop not only the Seaport of Singapore but to transform Singapore into an 'International Maritime Hub', which is complemented by the comprehensive eco-system of logistics, shipping, finance and legal services. The Chapter offers planners, policy makers and investors a structured framework of analysis to look into possible questions and the appropriate policies on seaport and maritime matters of global interest. Going forward, the key concerns include the global network of seaports associated with

Singapore, and the wider context of Singapore's relationship with the global maritime community as an international maritime centre. As Singapore continues to grow sustainably, there is likely to be pressure to limit further allocation of land for seaport and airport developments in favour of other higher yielding commercial and industrial real estate uses. Much progress has been made hitherto, be it in terms of design of seaports, the deployment of automation in various stages of cargo handling, or the exploitation of contemporary IT solutions for operational controls or business analytics. It is however noted that in the final analysis, the decisions are not answers to some economic questions. They should be guided by the strategic considerations of the overall competitiveness of Singapore.

Chapter 2 is concerned with risk management that has been demonstrated with Jurong Port as the case study. A uniquely formulated theoretical framework of analysis provides the basis for the identification of risks in determining Jurong Port's strategic options for growth. Two major categories of risks confronting Jurong Port are identified. The first is the uncertainty in the prediction of future rates of increase in seaport tariffs, the volumes of the various markets (businesses), and the implication of the rising trend in cargo containerisation. All these are exogenous factors that are mostly uncontrollable. The second is the risk relating to the internal weaknesses of Jurong Port like costing, pricing and the operating systems, that if not adequately addressed, will affect Jurong Seaport's competitiveness. Hence, there are basically two investment strategies for Jurong Port to choose from, namely, to become a full-fledged container terminal (i.e. Scenario 1) or to configure itself as a maritime industrial and logistics park (MILP) (i.e. Scenario 2). These strategies are subject to quantitative simulations, which are conducted by scrutinising the variability of the projected returns of the investment for each scenario, through the Monte Carlo risk simulation model. Furthermore, constraint optimisation under the non-linear algorithm is employed to determine the resources to be allocated among the potential cargo markets. The results affirm the Monte Carlo model simulations with respect to returns on investment.

The results indicate that although the projected returns of the "MILP" is not as impressive as the "container terminal" strategy, nevertheless, the variability of the former strategy's returns and hence the risks, are very much lower than those of the latter strategy. Therefore, the MILP strategy is recommended for Jurong Port and this will enable the Port to secure a firm foundation with respect to the localised industries, and to entrench its hub operations.

In drawing on the above recommendations, a sense of reality in view of Jurong Port's small size and limited capacity is to be taken into consideration. Significant innovations accompanied by major investments have been proposed to revitalise an otherwise aging national estate. By way of repackaging and rebranding it as the MILP rather than as a pure container terminal for obvious reasons of competence and strategic 'wholesomeness' of the former, should ultimately generate new demands and lift Jurong Port onto a new and high path of growth. Accordingly, the hosting of value-adding, processing and industrial activities, of the regional distribution centre and warehousing, have been identified as necessary compliments to reduce the elasticity of the otherwise extremely elastic and competitive transhipment business[9]. Furthermore, it is sensible to question the rationale for Singapore to focus only on container traffic particularly in the light of the countries in the region being inclined to handle their own domestic cargoes. Jurong Port's sustained viability may well be to redirect its resources and efforts to transform itself into the MILP while keeping a constant look out for niche opportunities to secure container traffic for e.g. through the structuring of "back-to-back agreements", covering terms like throughput guarantees and the exclusive use of Jurong Port with global shipping lines.

Chapter 3 recognises that seaport capacity expansion can be deemed to be an attractive, planned urban development policy for many seaports in the developing economies. From the direct

---

[9] Hutchison Seaport Holdings (HPH) which is the world's largest privately owned container terminal operator, adopts a policy of not investing in facilities that rely on transhipment (Brevetti, 1996).

real estate (DRE)perspective, Seaports are often invested and used like other large physical land infrastructure assets like highways to stimulate the economic development of a region or to promote the appreciation of DRE capital values (CVs) in the vicinity of seaports. It is believed that to some extent, the demand for physical land infrastructure or seaports is supply driven. As a consequence, competition between different regions of the same country or of competing economies in a particular region of the world have each intensified in recent years. Competition is also being fuelled as more and more seaports are being privatised in recent years.

However, without careful planning, the seaport capacity expansions may lead to financial difficulties in the long term, if the projected seaport throughput and revenue growth do not materialize. In the context of urban planning and development, failed seaport development projects due to abandonment before completion, may well lead to the dereliction of land and worse still, urban degeneration associated with the growth of urban slums. Before any expansion is undertaken, due diligence has to be done to obtain a realistically anticipated future seaport throughput and profitability of the desired expansion. Care should also be taken to evaluate the opportunity costs, resulting from such land-use zoning, as the opportunity costs will have long term repercussions. Chapter 3 has developed a rigorous and robust DPPM model on a reasonably sized and simplified scale. In particular, the DPPM is validated with scenarios 1 and 2 depicting the extremes of doing nothing and aggressively expanding to catch up with projected demand, which was projected at 60 mil twenty feet equivalent unita (TEU) per year in 10 years' time. The robustness of the DPPM is also verified with a sensitivity test adoting scenario 3, which pursues a modest expansion strategy, thereby projecting a throughput at an intermediate level of 40 mil TEU/year in 10 years' time. The DPPM when extended to take a close look at the Seaport of Hong Kong, offers meaningful insights into how the Seaport of Hong Kong may well be able to respond to changing market conditions and emerging competition as well as to play a sustained role in the future.

The wide-ranging policy formula that has given the Seaport of Hong Kong great success in the past i.e. good infrastructure, efficient operations, effective management, a free Seaport status, a well-defined legal system, well-established financial and business services, to name a few - should continue to offer the Hong Kong economy and its Seaport with a competitive edge. However, this policy formula is clearly not enough going forward, nor is it prudent for infrastructure planning and development in the Hong Kong and the neighbouring Shenzhen area to proceed in an uncoordinated manner. This approach may eventually lead to a destructive form of competition, to the detriment of all the parties concerned. Furthermore, it is also not desirable to have too many seaports within the same region without the supporting logistics ecosystem like warehousing, consolidation and distribution system, shipping connectivity, and other factors correspondingly addressed. Chapter 3 begins with the examination of the relationship between seaport throughput and capacity expansion. Subsequently, the DPPM is introduced as a rigorous alternative, which utilises the principles of system dynamics, to support *ex ante* scenario planning and policy analysis. It is hoped that Chapter 3 would provide planners, policy makers and investors a structured framework to examine possible questions and the appropriate policy decisions they would make. The DPPM can potentially be expanded to incorporate more factors and to deal with more complexities. It is hoped that the work of this Chapter would have provided a useful basis for further research in policy evaluation.

Chapter 4 reiterates that the late Sir Stamford Raffles, with great strategic foresight, had taken possession of the then unimportant and insignificant island state of Singapore. He envisaged that Singapore would become a significant trading port that would well serve the interests of Britain. His vision has largely panned out to be true. Today, Singapore is no longer a colony of Britain. Singapore is an interdependent sovereign island state. Britain is no longer a colonial master. Yet, both countries remain close friends and strategic partners whereby their future relationship would continue to be founded on their historical bond and shaped by the alignment of their strategic interests in the global new order. Indeed, the British maritime legacy in Singapore should not be confined to some maritime museums. Such a legacy should be leveraged upon as the basis to create value and improve the lives the peoples of both countries and globally. There is tremendous scope for public and private sectors' participation from both countries to form strategic and business alliances, based on the vision and the meaningful 'Framework for Strategic Maritime Collaboration'.

Lastly, Chapter 5 draws attention to financial instruments investing like that of common stocks, bonds, direct and indirect real estate, and the need that technical and fundamental analyses are often conducted to offer a reference for decision makers. Likewise, and in public physical infrastructure developments like the Singapore global Changi Airport, public funding is also a form of investment that entails uncertainties, which need to be rigorously evaluated with financial modelling on the risks and returns. Beyond financial returns, public physical infrastructural investing like Singapore's global Changi Airport seek to pursue a larger strategic objective for the long-term, well-being of the nation. In this regard, the Changi Airport is not just a public infrastructure, but also a key pillar of strength to support the growth of Singapore's trade-oriented market economy. Specifically, Singapore serves as the home base for another national institution like the ubiquitous Singapore Airlines (SIA), itself a market leader in the airline business.

Indeed, beyond airport development *per se*, the provision for the expansion of Singapore's global Changi Airport with its third and fourth runways, would eventuate significant contribution to Singapore's urban renewal and development. While the third runway would primarily be for civil aviation in conjunction with the development of terminal T5, the fourth runway would be for the eventual relocation of the RSAF Paya Lebar Air Base to the Changi East district. When the T5 and fourth runway developments materialise, this would free up some 800 ha of land, currently occupied by the RSAF Paya Lebar Air Base, is meant for housing, industry, recreation and other uses. The additional freed up land of 800 ha of land would enable Singapore's Urban Redevelopment Authority (URA) to liberalise the height restrictions around the Paya Lebar district, currently necessary to facilitate military air operations. Consequently, a lot of more urban redevelopment projects can be so planned and undertaken, to safeguard an even cleaner, greener, much less noisy, mixed-use built environment for Singaporeans; and to create more space for industrial and economic developments. Corresponding to these developments, the organisations that plan and execute the developments over the years have also evolved.

Prior to 2009, the Civil Aviation Authority of Singapore (CAAS) is the body in charge of developments and operations of airports in Singapore. Thereafter, the business aspects of the CAAS is corporatized to form the Changi Airport Group (CAG). Beyond managing the Changi Airport *per se*, CAG also invests in and manages foreign airports through its subsidiary Changi Airports International (CAI). CAI's goal is to build a quality portfolio of airport investments worldwide with strong markets and significant development potential. Key CAI business activities include investments in airports, the provision of consultancy and airport management services. Today, CAI's presence covers major economies like that for China, India, the Middle East and Europe. It is imperative that the investment appraisal and assessment of the Singapore global Changi Airport has to be based on a combination of financial analysis with strategic and business considerations. Chapter 5 has demonstrated how the development of the airport performance model (APM) on the basis of economic conceptions and the principles of system modelling can be readily adopted to support scenario planning and policy analysis. The airport performance model (APM) and Chapter 5 would be beneficial to policy makers and investors by providing them with a structured framework to consider the questions they are seeking to answer, and the decisions that they would need to make. It is acknowledged that the APM can potentially be expanded to include more factors, and to deal with more complexities. It is hoped that the work in this Chapter offers a preliminary platform to stimulate research endeavours in public policy analysis, especially in projecting future performance of physical transport infrastructural provision, within the context of portfolio management and its resource constrained optimisation. Beyond that, actual economic data can also be inputted into such models for scenarios generation to support policy development and decision making. Such big data analysis and scenario planning should open up a wide field for policy research, by way of reinforcing loop(s) to contribute towards making Singapore a knowledge and research centre for the aviation and aerospace sector.

www.ingramcontent.com/pod-product-compliance
Lightning Source LLC
Chambersburg PA
CBHW031049180526
45163CB00002BA/745